EXPLORING
THE LEVELS OF
CREATION

Also by Sylvia Browne

EXPLORING
THE LEVELS OF
CREATION

SYLVIA BROWNE

HAY HOUSE, INC.
Carlsbad, California
London • Sydney • Johannesburg
Vancouver • Hong Kong • New Delhi

Published and distributed in the United States by: Hay House, Inc. •
Published and distributed in Australia by: Hay House Australia Pty. Ltd. •
Published and distributed in the United Kingdom by: Hay House UK, Ltd. •
Published and distributed in the Republic of South Africa by: Hay House
SA (Pty), Ltd. • *Distributed in Canada by:* Raincoast • *Published in India by:*
Hay House Publications (India) Pvt. Ltd. • *Distributed in India by:* Media Star

Editorial supervision: Jill Kramer • *Design:* Jenn Tanzer

ISBN 13: 978-1-4019-0891-1
ISBN 10: 1-4019-0891-8

Printed in the United States of America

To my precious grandchildren . . .
Angelia, William, and Jeffrey

Contents

PREFACE

This book, like all of my works, came about because of several factors. First of all, it's the direct result of the curiosity—and the ensuing questions—of the thousands upon thousands of individuals I've read for over the years. It has also come out of research garnered from hundreds of people telling me about their life experiences and lessons. Then there's always my spirit guide Francine, who has been with me my entire life and has always been so helpful in "filling in the blanks."

Many people confuse spirit guides with angels. Well, angels are a separate creation of God that do not incarnate (nor do we ever become angels). This doesn't mean that they're any better than we are, they simply have a different calling and purpose. Angels are God's army of protection and assistance and were created to be helpers to humankind. All of us have specific angels assigned to us, and we can call on more at any time for additional needs in a given situation. (For more information on angels, please see my *Book of Angels*.) Spirit guides, on the other hand, are the kindred souls who were once incarnated on Earth and are now with us specifically to help us perfect, as Francine does for me.

To this day, everyone in the Sylvia Browne Corporation is a little paranoid about quoting Francine. That's because she related to me more than 60 years ago that if I ever used her words for my own gain, my psychic ability would be taken away. So when

I'm quoting her, I always ask her to please correct me if I don't present the correct verbiage of what she's conveyed to me audibly or through trance. I do know that she's been of great help to me, and the knowledge she imparts has been one of the cornerstones of my organization's philosophy.

Let me be very clear here: Most of the information you're going to read in these pages (or have read in my other books) was not volunteered by Francine. On the contrary, the ministers of my Gnostic church, the Society of Novus Spiritus, and I will keep getting a particular question asked of us. When it gets to be almost overwhelming, only then will I go into trance so that my spirit guide can come in and give us the answer.

I don't think that any of us would even think of some of these questions unless others constantly asked *us*. It's amazing and almost telepathic that these queries come in clumps or sections. It's almost as if something greater than we are (hasn't there always been?) is trying to get this information across. It's not that we haven't known about the levels of creation—in my other books, I've touched on them briefly, but it's nothing like the information we've begun to individually amass.

In my *Journey of the Soul* series, I mentioned the levels that the soul attained when we go Home to the Other Side and even how many lives we choose to reach the level we wish to attain. However, very little is known about the lower levels of creation, or the "underworld," so I had to do a lot of research to get information about them. I can tell you that researching not only the upper seven levels but the seven lower ones really answers so many questions about our mythology and even the nightmares we have . . . but I don't want to get ahead of myself.

When I began to lecture or even write, I'd encounter people who were searching, but with almost a low level of pessimism or the more simplified attitude of "What's the use?"—folks who were soul-sick and tired and, even worse, confused about life and death. So I decided that, controversial or not, I was going to let the world know what my ministers and I knew. Why keep the truth a secret? The glorious part about Gnosticism is that from its earliest inception, it has grown from constantly obtained knowledge. I don't mean to imply that the knowledge isn't or wasn't always there; rather, it has grown because the more questions we ask, the more answers are revealed to us. It's like on the Other Side where we never stop researching or discovering. That's one of the reasons I keep writing—not only do I feel the need to share our vast archives of knowledge with all of you, but it also seems that everything we reveal just elicits more questions . . . and then we're off on the investigation for more discoveries and truths.

I love writing about God, for my life is dedicated to Him, but it is truly an unending process. You see, as I learn more about God, I have the inroads through my wonderful publisher, Hay House, to always upgrade or add information about Him as I get it. It's truly a win-win situation: I get to put out what I've found for my readers and publish another book, while Hay House continues to build its legacy as the leading publisher of inspirational and spiritual books in the world. So even though much of what I'm about to tell you might seem familiar or repetitive if you've read my other works, know that Francine and I have revisited it all to give you the very latest information we have. I always want to let you know what I'm finding out . . . so let's get started.

❧❧ ❧❧

INTRODUCTION

Humankind has always wondered about creation. To say that it's perhaps the biggest mystery of all is the understatement of all understatements. There are nothing but questions as far as creation is concerned. You only have to look up at the night sky to have them start: Where did the vastness of the universe come from? Why is it so large? How many stars are up there? Who made all this? The inquiry can be endless, and humankind and its science has come up with very few answers so far.

The human mind is a marvelous and wonderful thinking mechanism, but it cannot even begin to comprehend the vastness and scope of creation. Just think about these few facts and see if your mind isn't totally blown away with the enormous and seemingly infinite area of space:

1. Our largest telescopes can only view a very small portion of the universe, yet what we do see are tens of thousands of galaxies that hold trillions of stars or suns and even more planets.

2. The Milky Way, in which our sun and solar system reside, is a small- to medium-sized galaxy. There are thousands out there that are larger, which our telescopes have picked up.

3. The nearest star system to us is a group of three stars called *Alpha Centauri*, which is approximately 4.3 light-years in distance from us.

4. A light-year is the distance that light travels in a year (in a vacuum), at about 186,000 miles per second. That's like circling our planet at the equator a little over seven times in one second.

5. Our sun is approximately 92,000,000 miles from Earth, and light travels that distance in about eight minutes. Earth is about 49,000,000 miles from Mars (depending upon how close our planet's orbit is to Mars). It would take a spacecraft traveling at 25,000 miles per hour about 81 days, or almost three months, to reach Mars, but light travels from Earth to Mars in a little over four minutes.

As you can see, the distances are astronomical (no pun intended). When you start to think that light travels at 186,000 miles per second and it takes it more than four light-years to reach the nearest star system, it boggles the mind to think about such a distance . . . and that's only to the *nearest* one! If you consider the billions of stars out there that are considerably farther away, you can't even begin to comprehend the enormity of the universe—especially when you can only see a small portion of it. So can you believe that there are people out there who either think that there *is* no God or that He's dead?

I hope that what I explain in this book will give you a deeper understanding of how our universe works and what we can aspire to. Knowledge sets us free, and I feel that it also brings us closer to God by giving us the understanding that everything has a purpose and a place.

The Schematics of Creation

There are several different dimensions that exist in creation—what we call "Earth" is only one of them, as is the dimension we call "the Other Side." (This is our Home, where we came from into life and where we go after death.)

As God's creations, we're like little atoms in comparison to the vastness of the universe, so how can we even begin to comprehend what it would take to *make* creation? Well, God tries to simplify things for our finite minds by giving us an outline of seven schematics. I'd now like to share that information with you, which Francine imparted to my ministers. The simplicity and order of it is perfection in itself and gives us a little more insight into our origins.

First Schematic: Creation of the Universe

Creation, according to our scientists, took billions of years and is constantly evolving and reinventing itself—star systems come and go, suns burn out or become supernovas, and there's constant movement in the universe as we know it. Yet while we humans are limited by time and space, God is not. Everything in creation is happening, has happened, and will be happening in God's *now.* There is no time, as far as God is concerned; and for Him, everything is happening simultaneously and encompasses past, present, and future. By just thinking about the enormity and vastness of creation and the power it took to create it, perhaps we can set our egos aside for a moment and concede that God isn't limited by time or space; indeed, He has no limitations at all.

The reason that the universe was created is fairly simple: to prepare a place—or, more accurately, billions of places—in which living creations could exist and inhabit. Just as when we have babies and want to give them a nice place to grow up, God wants the same thing for His children. I can't tell you *how* He created the universe, as even our best scientists and theologians don't know (and I doubt that we could understand a technical or scientific explanation anyway). So, for the purposes of comprehension for the layperson, just know that the universe was made in some way by God.

Through the creation of the universe (and this neither confirms nor denies "the big bang theory," for, regardless, it's all happening in God's now), God made sure that certain places would be hospitable for life as we know it. Such hospitable planets got into the correct orbit around whatever sun(s) to sustain life, and then went through volcanic and ice-age periods to prepare their surfaces for life. Our particular planet, Earth, was colonized from another inhabited one, but that's neither here nor there— the point is that some planets were made by God to sustain life. Vegetation, water, land, and earth and sea creatures were all made ready for the coming of humankind and the implementation of the second schematic.

Second Schematic: Creation of Entities

With hospitable planets now ready, the second part of God's giant plan of creation was implemented, and countless angels of all phyla came forth to aid His ultimate creations—us. Like tiny balls of energy and light coming out of a giant Divine sparkler, each of us carries an individual part of our Creator in the form of energy that contains a mind, spirit, and soul. Francine says we're told that we existed in these orbs of light for what would seem to us an eternity as the universe formed . . . but again, this was all happening simultaneously in God's now. Then came the next schematic.

Third Schematic: Entities Are Placed on Planets

Entities were then sent to individual planets (which didn't include Earth), in the form of almost cylindrical-like tubes of a silvery nature. Once upon the surface of a planet, the tubes opened to reveal physical bodies. Each tube had a male and female form within it, plastered together almost as in a cocoon. They then slowly peeled off from each other into separate bodies containing both male and female souls. All entities were created in duality as male and female soul mates as a reflection of the nature of God, which contains aspects of both the male ("Father God") and female ("Mother God," or "Azna").

Soul mates evolve separately and draw back toward each other, finally reaching each other in totality near the end of their individual evolvement. And you only have one soul mate—you were connected to each other in the beginning in your silvery chariot of creation and peeled apart to develop as an individual entity with your own free will to learn for God.

As you attain your own chosen level of evolvement, you come back together with your soul mate in a truly spiritual bond that's what we would call a "heavenly marriage." In the interim period, you usually see and interact with one another while on the Other Side. However, you usually don't incarnate with your soul mate, as that only happens in rare instances. The logic here is that the soul mate can protect you more while on the Other Side than it can while incarnate. As each of you evolves, you become closer, and not just in love—you also become more spiritually and mentally attuned to each other and again become almost like one, as you were in the beginning.

As with anything, there are some exceptions in which an entity chooses to go back into the uncreated mass of God rather than connect with their soul mate. In those very rare instances, we often see the soul mate also making that same choice, finding another mate, or just choosing not to have one at all. With so much to do and so many friends and loved ones around, the lack of a soul mate should never be viewed as a hardship.

As dark entities began to exert their agenda on the beginnings of creation, God changed the rules, so to speak, by enacting the next schematic to create other dimensions of existence. (For a complete explanation of dark entities, please see Chapter 18.)

Fourth Schematic: Creation of Other Dimensions

As life on the initial planets became more difficult for positive or "white" entities (which is what most of us are) due to the advent of negativity and evil, physical death became a reality. The story of Cain and Abel in Genesis is an analogy to indicate this rise of negativity and evil, for God marked Cain for all time so that others wouldn't kill him, and he was sent to wander the earth. This is an analogy for separating positive white entities from the negative dark ones in a true reality.

God created a new reality as the old one became tainted with negativity. He created the Other Side for all the white entities to have as a sanctuary and didn't allow *any* evil to enter that new reality. God also created additional dimensions for other creations, which we know now as "the underworld." (Please see Part I for a closer look.) The old reality of the original planets was no more and became a transitory plane of existence. Death was a by-product of this transitory plane because of the horrible actions perpetrated by dark entities.

The new dimension of the Other Side became the true reality for all of the white souls of creation, where they could reside forever in God's love and protection. The Other Side's perfect environment of love and happiness was, in a way, the instigation for the next schematic of reincarnation. You see, all the original areas that were used initially for our place of residence became transitory learning spots only.

Now just as our planet, Earth, has its own Other Side, where everything of beauty and nature is duplicated, so do other planets have their *own* Other Sides in which the beauty and nature of their individual planets is duplicated. In fact, Francine has told me numerous times about magnificent places on other planets that she's visited. She's assured me that when we go back Home, many of us visit these worlds to see such wondrous acts of creation.

God in His love for us has made safe and wondrous havens throughout the universe for us to live in and enjoy. A perfect environment of love, peace, and harmony is one in which evil and negativity don't exist—so in order for us to learn about them, the next schematic had to be enacted.

Fifth Schematic: Reincarnation

Reincarnation is a subject that I love to talk and teach about, but it wasn't always that way. As I've related in other books, I didn't always believe in this premise or even care about it one way or the other. However, my beloved Grandma Ada was a strong believer in reincarnation (as was her entire family), and as I got older, she and I started having more "adult" conversations. I usually initiated them with my endless questions; and my grandmother and I would talk endlessly about subjects such as Atlantis, aliens, spirit guides, heaven, religion, and God—so it was inevitable that the conversation would eventually get around to reincarnation. I was very skeptical, though, and although I saw the logic of many of Grandma Ada's arguments, I didn't embrace the philosophy of reincarnation all that much. It wasn't that I disbelieved . . . it was more that I really didn't care about it.

I was a voracious reader, so my grandmother introduced me to some books on the subject. I read all about Bridey Murphy and other cases in which reincarnation was in evidence, and I was somewhat intrigued. Yet it wasn't until I was practicing hypnosis on someone who "flipped" (my term for a person in hypnosis who suddenly goes to a past life) on me that I became utterly fascinated and poured myself into research on reincarnation. I am now a firm believer and know that it does in fact exist. I've done thousands of past-life regressions and have checked on a good number of them, and I've found them to be accurate in every detail. Some I couldn't find the information to verify, but I *was* able to confirm so many that my skepticism vanished.

Reincarnation is the tool that God gave us to help us learn. By being able to live multiple lives, we can subject ourselves to many more facets of negativity than one life could give us. Reincarnation explains the inequities in life, such as why one person can die very young and another lives to be very old, why some are rich and some are poor, and why some are disabled and others aren't. The list goes on and on. With our free will, we pick the lives we want to live, so we may choose to be poor in one life and rich in another. We all try to become as well rounded as possible, so the chances that you've lived a life in abject poverty are as high as having lived one of wealth. We've all existed in different areas of the world and in all kinds of cultures and racial backgrounds. If you're white, you've probably lived as a black, Asian, or Indian; if you're black, you've lived as a white; and so on and so forth. We subject ourselves to all that this planet has to offer for the one purpose of incarnation—to learn for our soul and for God.

Sixth Schematic: Incarnating on Other Planets

Again, for the finite mind's understanding, this is the schematic that we now exist in. (Both the fifth and sixth schematics are interwoven together for the premise of learning, and most of us now on the Earth plane have lived on other planets as well.)

Francine continually tells me that life on this planet is the toughest test there is. Only entities with courage and perseverance choose to incarnate on Earth because it is, as I like to call it, the insane asylum of the universe. It's the ultimate post-graduate school, where you get your "Ph.D. in soul evolvement." To show you how tough it is, a large part of creation won't even come near this place, let alone incarnate on it. (I've personally incarnated on this planet 54 times, and I've decided that I'm either stupid or a glutton for punishment.)

The reason we incarnate on other worlds is to get a different perspective on evil and negativity. Some planets hardly have any evil or negativity, while others like Earth are rampant with it. Some places are more highly evolved when it comes to technology and their treatment of fellow creations, while others are more primitive in nature, again like Earth. Souls incarnating on different planets then get a different viewpoint: Some see how certain worlds have basically conquered their negative emotions, others see those where emotions are almost nonexistent and intellect reigns supreme, while still others see those that are highly emotional (such as Earth) but more orderly in nature.

With billions of inhabited planets, you can find almost any scenario you'd want and experience it for your own soul's knowledge and evolvement. When this schematic that we're now in ends, the final one of God will take effect.

Seventh Schematic: Merging All of Creation Together

The final schematic of God is the one that all of us are looking forward to. This is the scenario of merging all of the dimensions of true reality—that is, all the Other Sides in creation to one dimension of reality, where harmony, peace, happiness, and love exist in the magnificence of God. The Other Sides on all the planets are miniature representations of that final dimension now, but the sheer magnitude of it will be something to behold.

Can you even imagine it? I don't think I can. Everything evil or negative will be gone, reabsorbed back into the Godhead. Those of us who have chosen to love God and have battled negativity and evil for so long won't have to fight anymore. The universe will no longer be needed as a school to learn in and will either be reabsorbed or saved for another purpose.

In the seventh schematic, we'll live in a reality of impossible beauty and love. It will be our home and paradise to live in for all eternity and will never cease to exist. We'll never have to be born and die in an incarnation ever again. We'll be able to learn, study, and play to our heart's content, basking in the wonder and sheer exquisiteness of God's glorious and awe-inspiring love.

Now that I've touched on how the universe is ordered, I'd like to take a minute to discuss the rest of the book. As I've already mentioned, Part I takes a look at the lower levels of creation, or the underworld. Part II explains the seven levels of life on the Earth plane, while Part III also explores seven levels—those of the Other Side. Finally, Part IV gives you some new information on a few subjects I've tackled several times in the past, but it was really fun for me to revisit these old favorites and "freshen them up" a bit, if you will.

As you read, always keep in mind that, even though I've researched the subjects included herein thoroughly, these are still *my* findings. I hope that you'll explore and study further for your own sake, taking with you what you truly believe in. Never accept something *anyone* says whole hog—unless it truly resonates with you, too.

Having said that, let's start exploring all the wondrous levels of creation!

PART I

EXPLORING THE UNDERWORLD

INTRODUCTION
TO PART I

The subject I'd like to examine in this part is one I've never discussed (at least in depth) in any other book: the underworld.

Just as the Other Side exists in a dimension with a higher vibrational level than Earth has, so does there exist one with a *lower* vibrational level. Now I know that some of you may find these lower levels to be as far-fetched as I did when I first heard about them. But at the risk of sounding like I'm completely off my rocker, I've come to believe that everything we humans have created (or even imagined) exists somewhere, so why wouldn't this be true of the underworld, too?

Imagination has to be one of the worst words in the English language, for it implies something that isn't real. I contend that there is no such thing as imagination, for if the mind can bring an image of something up, then it truly exists. The mind, therefore, is simply bringing forth a memory.

For example, if I asked you to summon up an image of a wang-doodle into your mind, you couldn't because you don't know what a wang-doodle is. But if I told you that a wang-doodle is a small animal with big round ears, long orange fur, a tiny nose, pointy teeth, little claws, and no tail, you could probably bring a similar image to mind. And the more of a description I gave you, the more precise your image would be. I don't mean that we'd actually be creating a wang-doodle as we did this, but we *would* be drawing on our memories of certain things to conjure up an image. In other words, we all know what "small" is, what "big round ears" look like, what "orange fur" is, and so forth.

As far as creatures in the underworld go, we may have seen something similar in a movie or book, so it isn't hard to see how many of these lower-level dwellers came into being. As I explained in my book *Secrets & Mysteries of the World,* such "tulpas" can become real. Since thoughts are things that carry energy, when that energy is expressed in a belief that's strong enough and given out by many, it can change its form and become a real thing. Prayer can do the same in the form of miracles, and positive thinking can lead to a healthier body and more success in life. Take this a bit further in the form of a belief in folklore and mythology, and creation takes place . . . which is why these lower levels exist.

The underworld is not a geographical place per se, but it *is* ruled by Lilith. Even though tradition gives her somewhat of a bad slant, she's actually a very advanced being especially created to rule the lower levels of creation. She relates solely to Azna, the Mother God. (It isn't that God the Father is ever left out because He is the one Who holds everything and everyone in place.) So this ultimately means that all of the creations I'm about to examine in the next several pages aren't just the product of our beliefs and thoughts— rather, God may just have had a hand in the process as well.

❧◦❧

CHAPTER 1

A BRIEF RUNDOWN
OF THE LEVELS

Throughout history, every culture has told of their "little people," such as the Menehunes of Hawaii, the leprechauns of Ireland, the elves of Germany's Black Forest, or even the tooth fairy of many cultures. There has to be some reason why people have kept these ancient stories alive through written or oral tradition.

Personally, I think that knowing about the lower levels is just for information, and you should keep your mind in your own dimension. Many of these areas of the underworld are for children anyway, as this is where they see fairies, gnomes, flying horses, unicorns, and the like. (After all, children *are* psychic.) Keep in mind that just as we rarely see the inhabitants of the Other Side, we also don't tend to witness the creations that exist in the underworld. Nevertheless, I'd like to explain each of the seven levels and their inhabitants, one by one.

The First Level—Fairies, Nymphs, Sprites, and Devas

The first level of the lower levels is the highest and contains fairies, nymphs, sprites, and devas. Fairies and sprites live in the woods and glens; water nymphs reside in streams, lakes, and ponds; and devas are sentient, making up and residing in trees and all living matter. (The old idiom of knocking on wood comes from waking the devas for good luck.) My own grandmother prayed to the devas of her garden and plants, and I swear that she could put a stick in the ground and have it grow. I mean she didn't just have a green thumb . . . her whole hand was green. Her gardens were awesome, with vegetables at least twice the size of others in the vicinity and flowers that would bloom and bloom, with huge blossoms and spectacular hues.

Most cultures appear to accept devas—even Sanskrit scrolls verify that the Tibetans believed in them. In fact, *deva* means "being of brightest light," or "nature spirits," in Sanskrit. It seems that these creatures are content in *being*, while we humans are concerned about *doing*. And they're always willing to help us if we simply let them.

The lower phylum of deva resides in inanimate objects such as rocks or even machinery. (I've known people who really understood this and talked to their cars, stoves, saws, and washing machines and begged them to work—and more times than not, they did.)

You can find a lot of lore on these first-level inhabitants in American Indian and Hawaiian cultures, both loving and revering the land and the little people who coexist with it. Also, note that the entities on this level seem to be very friendly toward, and caring about, humankind, as they tend to our children and even animals.

The Second Level—Gnomes and Elves

Dwellers of the second level have been given good as well as bad PR. While gnomes are a help to human and plant life, they're more interested (as are the elves) in keeping to themselves and taking care of the forests and the minerals of the earth. Unlike the beautiful sprites, fairies, and nymphs, gnomes look old and gnarled and seem to be gruff and not particularly fond of people or animals. However, they have been known to help sick animals in the forest if no one else is around.

Elves, on the other hand, have their consciousness deep in Mother Nature and dwell in mountains and forests, and near streams. They can also shy away from humans but aren't as curmudgeonly as gnomes (who might be synonymous with the Irish leprechauns). Elves have been known to leave presents for underprivileged children (as in Santa Claus and his helpers) and help people with tasks in their homes. In fact, literature abounds with these stories, such as *The Elves and the Shoemaker* by the Brothers Grimm, in which an old cobbler was too tired to finish all the shoes that people ordered, so elves came in and finished the job for him during the night.

In folklore, it was often said that gnomes or elves (and even beloved fairies) would steal babies. This, of course, isn't true and was probably something that got told to mask kidnappings by other humans. Elves and gnomes do give spiritual support to all plant life, since this is where they live, but they try to stay as invisible as possible.

The Third Level—Giants and Dragons

Giants and dragons exist in mythology (as do all the other residents of the underworld) and are steeped in folklore. Of course the Bible has the famous story of David and the giant Goliath, and we also read about St. George who slayed the dragon. Both giants and dragons seem to be kind creatures connected to mountainous territory that have been given a bad rap. It has been reported that giants reside in ancient forests to this day. (Might Bigfoot be one?) In addition, such creatures are gentle and have been seen by very sensitive people, and not just in dreams.

Dragons have always been renowned for having great strength; in fact, they're supposedly able to transfer their power to humans at will. Lesser dragons exist solely to project lust and power, but the higher ones have been known to cure illness. Dragons have been seen floating high over the cloud level in all kinds of vivid colors and don't seem to descend into the lower atmospheres—although at one time they did walk the earth, which may have been at the same time as dinosaurs. They seem to be a reservoir of energy for the planet, and some groups even think that they protect the atmosphere and the very air we breathe.

The Fourth Level—Unicorns and Flying Horses

The home of unicorns and flying horses (such as Pegasus) is also the first of what are often called the "nightmare levels." I think the reason might be because these horses ("mares") would tend to be seen at night, so they'd be "night mares."

According to fable or folklore, the unicorn has only been tamed or caught by a virgin, and it reputedly has magical powers. The mythical winged horse appears to have been around as a type of messenger from heaven. There must be some truth to this because Francine has said that she's seen it, and I can tell you from being with her almost 70 years that she's never given in to any kind of weird fantasy (in fact, in some ways she's more pragmatic and skeptical than I am—which is saying a lot). We also see flying horses in television commercials or in the logo for a movie production company, as they represent freedom and beauty.

The Fifth Level—Centaurs, Cyclopes, Goblins, and Sorcerers

Now we come to an interesting level in the underworld—"the barrier level," in which strict containment is enacted by Lilith. This is also the first level where we find creations that are made by humans, not God. To that end, we find many mythological creatures here, such as centaurs (half man and half horse), Cyclopes (giants with one eye), and goblins.

As for the so-called wizards, true sorcerers, warlocks, and witches that inhabit this level, they're not the nature-loving types who practice the ancient religion of Wicca that we know on our Earth plane, but the almost garish Hollywood types with pointed hats and broomsticks, like the Wicked Witch of the West in *The Wizard of Oz*. These are basically created tulpas, or human thoughtforms made into substance. As I mentioned before, everything that human beings have thought, believed in, or made up in our imagination has a place in some reality—even if it does exist on a lower level. Humankind can think something into existence, but the actual entity can't leak into our dimension because Lilith, the strong keeper of the underworld, blocks them.

I'm sure that's how the early Romans and Greeks came up with a lot of their mythology. Someone, whether it was a high priestess or oracle, tuned in to the lower levels. I'm also convinced that many fantasy writers have tapped in to these levels from time to time for inspiration. An example of this would almost surely be J.R.R. Tolkien and his wonderful books on orcs, goblins, and hobbits, with wizards and magic thrown in.

The Sixth and Seventh Levels—"Mind-Dump Areas"

Now we reach what are known as the "mind-dump areas" of the underworld. Here's where we find "the bogeyman," the so-called devil, the Loch Ness monster (or any number of what we may term *monsters*), and the like. I'm sure the reason that our dreams are disturbed by these bizarre creatures is because we subconsciously bring them up.

Francine says that hardly anyone visits these levels—it's more or less just our thoughtforms that dwell within these realms. They can't leak upward, and for all practical purposes we can't descend to them. The beings that reside here are probably in our mind from studying about them on the Other Side or even hearing about them in this life. Movies, books, and TV shows bring them to our awareness, as do the countless fairy tales, myths, and stories that are handed down from generation to generation.

There's no way that this subconscious knowledge is like that of past-life "bleed-throughs"—for example, the reason that you can't stand anything tight around your neck is because in a past life you were hung, or the pain in your back that no one can diagnose stems from your back being broken in a past life, and so forth. Just as we bring over great knowledge and talents from our previous existences, we can also carry painful memories with us, but this has nothing to do with the mind-dump areas.

Because these creations are on such a low level, they can't materialize—not even in thoughtform do they become real. It's almost as if humankind can summon types of bizarre thoughts (sexual as well as sadistic and masochistic), and they all reside there. I personally believe that *every* evil notion resides there . . . as they'd logically have to if it were a sort of storage house for the thoughts of creation.

It would seem to me that the sixth and seventh levels would also contain thoughts that are pleasant and funny yet without any real purpose. With all this melding of contradictory, chaotic, lovely, *and* bizarre mind creations, it's no wonder that hardly anyone ever visits these levels. These areas are probably what our definition of utter chaos would be, with confusion and discordance running rampant with beauty and harmony, as a constant barrage of emotion and feelings rain down. Who wants that?

I think that's why Francine was reluctant to divulge this information until I kept after her to tell me. She assured me that Lilith (with the guardianship of Mother God, of course) doesn't ever let these lower levels leak up, and that's certainly understandable. Please be aware that we can have knowledge of these types of places, but since they don't affect us at all, they're really of no concern. Now the five upper levels of the underworld *are* privy to our world, but they rarely leak through and are no threat to us. Fairies, gnomes, little people, unicorns, and the like are not harmful to humankind and many times help children and animals, as well as us grown-ups. They're not to be confused with the Other Side's angels and spirit guides, nor with ghosts—these are more what the ancients referred to as the "mythology levels" . . . except they're not myths.

It's very easy for humankind to be afraid of "evil" or brand anything we don't understand as such. It's just like thinking that there are demons and a devil. There are confused and mischievous ghosts who don't like us inhabiting their space or domain, but they're certainly not evil. In all my life (and I've been to thousands of hauntings in the U.S. and in almost any country you can think of), I haven't found a single evil spirit. I *have* found entities who don't know that they're dead or who are confused and agitated, but never evil.

I'm sure that the reason religion takes a dim view of certain advanced spiritual beings is because it feels that they take away from God. But how can they? There is God the Father and the Mother and our beloved Lord; the other lesser phylum such as angels, humankind, Lilith, and her domain; and even the lowest levels that are on their own vibrational level or dimension of existence. Creation is what it is—and only God knows the all of it. If for no other reason, these lower levels are valid because humankind keeps reporting on their existence, whether in stories, songs, or dreams.

I hope that this chapter has helped to explain some of our bizarre nightmares. As I stated earlier, our subconscious probably has this knowledge stored because we researched the underworld on the Other Side or encountered such creatures during a past life in a simpler time. But regardless of how we became aware of this knowledge, it's basically for informational purposes to explain some of the unexplainable. So to those of you who have seen these creatures (as I have), don't despair and think that you're going crazy . . . it's just another little corner of our vast creation, and it truly does exist.

Chapter 2

Additional Information from Francine

While we're on the subject of the underworld, I'd like to stop here and insert what Francine once came up with in a trance session, which I recently found in our archives. It's a trifle long, but I think that you'll find it as fascinating as I did. It also shows you the wide scope of research my ministers and I have done over the years, as well as how much information our archives hold on various subjects. Interspersed throughout this trance session are questions from the research group, which are in italics.

Research Trance with Francine—February 2, 1990

The seven lower levels of creation are quite fascinating. These are the ones that all thought resides in, some of which invades your dreamlike states, such as monsters and other grotesque things. The levels are backed up to each other, and you have seven of them accelerating upward on the Other Side. The higher the level, the more accelerated the soul; but on the lower levels of creation, the first is the most accelerated and the seventh is lowest. It's a mirrored image. Level 1 is where your wonderful sprites, fairies, nymphs, and devas reside—they're really a subculture. In this country [the U.S.], if you start talking about this place where fairies dwell, you're going to run into people who think that you're really crazy. But you're not going to tell anybody in the British Isles that they don't exist. In fact, most of the Celtic countries believe in what they call "the little people"—they're fairies, sprites, and nymphs; and they're beautiful.

Lilith is the governess of that level of the sprites. It's terrible because she was touted as being the "queen of the witches," and that was ignorance. It was said that she's a woman of darkness, and she isn't! She's very close to Azna (Mother God); and she's a beautiful, wonderful entity.

Inhabitants of the first four levels do come to our Other Side, but they don't have to—and the lower the level, the more infrequent their visits. They can stay in their own dimension for as long as your Earth dimension lasts, and then when all the dimensions eventually merge, everyone will join with us on the Other Side. They don't have the adversity to overcome that those who live on your planet do. I think that's why when an entity lives a life on the Earth plane, the span of years is shorter. You have so much adversity that it just wears you down—if you had totally happy, wonderful surroundings, you'd probably live much longer. But the creations on the lower levels don't have any schematic of perfection. They're very much like animals, perfect in their own origins of creation. They don't have miserliness, greed, and other problems to overcome. They live in an almost perfect environment.

Q: Do they reincarnate and change species?

A: No. They keep their phylum perfect. Lilith will always stay the way she is—she'll never advance to a level of human, but she *is* an entity directly from God who belongs to His own species derivatives.

Q: *Can Lilith help us in life?*

A: Oh yes, absolutely. Unlike us [spirit guides], Lilith and the creations on the upper levels of the underworld can more readily cross dimensions. That's why every once in a while, individuals will see the little people more than they do spirits because they're closer to the same vibrational level as the Earth plane. Over in some countries they actually leave food out for these little people . . . and they come and take it!

Being the queen of the fairies, Lilith can be very powerful. The only one we know Who really converses with her is Mother God. However, I know for a fact that Sylvia can speak to her—she got in contact with Lilith at one point in her life, but being so reasonable she dropped it. *You* can get in touch with Lilith, too. She's absolutely magnificent, going about the world doing wondrous good deeds. Her main focus is to take care of children. She has been very busy and in somewhat of a mess and distraught lately with all these missing kids, which is almost like an epidemic.

So if you're dealing with any children who might be in trouble—I don't care what age they are—appeal to Lilith because she's the "beloved one of children."

Q: *What is Lilith's purpose?*

A. Protection. The tragedy is that you have so much protection around you and you've never known that you could call on it. It's like somebody dropped you on this planet without giving you a map of where the gullies and dark forests were or where you'd run into the trolls of life. This is the worst part about life—you're thrown into a foxhole with a dead radio, and every time you stick your head out, you get shot at.

Nevertheless, there are all kinds of entities you can call on. You could have a fortress around you that nothing could penetrate!

Q: *Can we appeal to Lilith and her domain for lost animals?*

A. Yes, try to, because she's been known to bring animals back. If you ask her to solve that for you, you might be very surprised at how powerful she is.

Q: *How do these entities protect us?*

A. They create a pushing effect. For example, several years ago Sylvia had to do a haunting investigation at the Winchester Mystery House in San Jose, California. She was scheduled to do a séance, and as she always does, she said, "I don't want to know anything that's going on. Set up the room and I'll come in." She was put in an inner courtyard while they got everything ready. Now this was after normal business hours, and what they didn't realize (or just forgot) was that a door on a time clock automatically sprung open the kennel of the resident guard dog. A huge German shepherd was suddenly let loose in the courtyard.

Sylvia was sitting on a bench with her then-husband and happened to look over to see this huge dog standing maybe 150 feet from her. Now many animals aren't really that sharp-sighted—most people think they are, but it's not until they get close to you that they sense you and sniff the air. This particular dog was very dangerous, so Sylvia told her husband not to move . . . and then she called me.

I was frantic because I was afraid that I wasn't on a low enough level to get to that animal, so I called Lilith, who *was* on the same level. Lilith grabbed that dog by the scruff of the neck and pulled it away, and then Sylvia and her husband ran inside. She said, "Francine, thank you so much!" She's always attributed this rescue to me—now she'll know that I wasn't the one who saved her.

If you're ever in a similar situation, please call on the lower-level entities to protect you. Especially if, let's say, you come across a mother bear with her cubs. There's no way that you could call your guide, as we might not be able to get to you. Your angels could probably push it off for a while, but the entity you really want to call is somebody on the same level.

So you see that there are levels of protection for you all over the place. Now you may wonder why Lilith wouldn't just know that you're in trouble. Well, these entities don't have a network to keep track of every single human being who's in trouble. But if you know enough to call their name, an electrical current is sent right to them like a siren, and they know that they're needed. They're not God, the same as we [spirit guides] aren't, so they can't always keep everyone in their focus. That's why it's marvelous to say, "Lilith, please—I'm standing here on this road and need help." Even just saying her name has more impact because you're closer to her level.

In addition to helping human beings, Lilith is sort of the St. Francis of the lower levels in that she protects animals. So if you have a cat or a dog that needs protection or is sick, I'd call on Lilith to attend to that animal. I don't care whether it's a horse or whatever it might be.

Q: *For whom are these lower levels experiencing?*

A. Their own selves. And I think the tragedy is that the more humankind builds and develops with their concrete and steel, the more these creations get pushed out of their habitats. There's the famous case in Ireland when they decided to build an airport runway at Shannon through some fairy rings. They had so many inexplicable accidents and delays that the local populace finally convinced the airport authorities not to destroy the rings. When the runway was built in another area, the accidents and delays stopped almost immediately.

Q: *Do these entities have bodies? Can they be photographed?*

A. Yes, they sleep, eat, and procreate, but they live in an environment that's almost totally devoid of greed, which is a perfect environment. And yes, they can be photographed (and have been).

Q: *Are there "little green men"?*

A. No. Seeing such apparitions indicates a drug-induced state, which means that the mind is conjuring up parts of things and putting them together, especially from the subconscious. The subconscious tends to fragment reality in dreams—you'll get the nose of an aardvark and the feet of a duck. The same thing happens when people in alcoholic binges see pink elephants—elephants and the color pink do exist, but what happens is that the mind fragments and does an overlay. That is how monsters are created. These are parts of things that exist and are pieced together to fit, and they create grotesqueness.

Q: *How do these lower-level entities know about us and our needs?*

A. Their life form is simpler. That's why an animal can spot a spirit faster than a human can. Have you ever watched a cat or dog bristle at something in a room and you have no idea why? It's because their eyes are unclouded! An animal, bird, or lower-level entity will know that a tornado or an earthquake is coming long before you will because of the innocence of the lower levels.

Animals don't have the levels of perfection to go through like the human entity does because the mind is simply sensate, such as: *I am hungry. I need to eat. I need to sleep. I need to procreate. I need to drink water. I will survive until I die.* There are higher levels, such as sprites, little people, nymphs, and the like that do have what we call "almost-sensate thinking minds," but they don't have pain, remorse, guilt, or all the other things that might be considered negative. They are good and are constantly attending to humans, as are the devas of nature and inanimate objects.

Q: Why would Lilith and other entities on the lower levels care about us?

A. In the underworld, the closer the level is to your own, the more ingrained and helpful the inhabitants are. The first four levels care in varying degrees, with the first one doing so most of all—and, of course, that's where Lilith resides. She's a message carrier who has great power, which she uses to help humankind and keep the lower levels contained.

Lilith is so very advanced that she can trilocate. She has great lateral movement and great power, and if she can't be somewhere, then she can and will send her consorts and followers.

Q: Can you elaborate a bit more on the upper four levels?

A. You might think that I'm given to fits of fantasy, but I honestly have seen the fairies, mermaids, and unicorns, and they're just beautiful. I saw a golden-hued dragon the other day that was absolutely spectacular.

Some of the four upper levels of the underworld even have what we call the "magicians," or the wonderful ones who created magic throughout the world. There is such a level of true beauty, as I've related, a wondrous fairyland type of atmosphere. Look at some of your ancient Oriental art, especially how they used the gorgeous dragons and beautiful monkey statues—all those are brought up from these beautiful first four levels. Even the three lower (particularly the last two) aren't all that bad, but that's where the waste goes from our minds. Nothing in God's time or place is destroyed anywhere.

Q: Do the two lowest levels include animal thoughts?

A. Yes, both animal thoughts and sensate feelings. Thoughts are things that have energy, and since nothing is destroyed, those thoughts have to reside somewhere. So where do you go but where your thoughts take you? The lowest levels would never hurt you, you can't get caught there, and nobody ever stays there for very long. Can you imagine the enormous amount of energy that would hit you like a furnace blast, carrying every emotion, both good and bad? I do think that people sometimes go down to these terrible levels and are convinced that it's where hell is because the thoughtforms then begin to take shape.

Q: Are those our nightmares?

A. To a certain degree, they can be the *cause* of some of your nightmares. If you're troubled, you can seep down to those levels in your sleep. Now the guardian of those levels is Lilith, and she can cement them closed—so if you're having trouble with nightmares, you can certainly petition her to close that "door." You don't have to keep seeping down to those levels. The more people become entrenched in the lower levels and the more negative they become, the closer they get to where thoughts become things.

Q: In near-death experiences, some people see a "hell." Are these the lower levels?

A. Absolutely. Not even the dark entities like to go there, so you can imagine that it's pretty unpleasant. What's also amazing is that the sky is very dark in the lower two levels. When I went in there, it was like an electrical storm going on above me all the time. I felt like I was in a giant brain, and it was very frightening . . . and very few things scare me. But no entities actually reside there, and we've never lost anyone who's visited.

No entity in the state of physiological makeup [life] should try to go to the lower two levels. It wouldn't hurt you, but you'd only go there once. Sometimes those in an astral state have their focus slip and they get caught in these two lower levels. Again, ask Lilith to close the door so that this doesn't happen to you.

This is also why children experience nightmares. They're such marvelously curious entities that they really don't want to be in their bodies—they're always out tripping around in an astral state. (Sylvia's youngest son, Christopher, almost drove us on the Other Side crazy when he was a child because he was always on the steps of the Hall of Wisdom, and I must have chased him away at least four or five times a week.) This is also frightening because a child can lose focus easily—they go into the lower levels and start playing with the fairies. This is why I say to stay on your own level! Yes, it's wonderful to believe in fairies and unicorns and all that, but the levels are supposed to be kept pure within themselves.

Q: Why do you call the sixth and seventh levels the "mind-dump areas"?

A. Well, what's strange about the lower two levels is that they contain mainly discarded thoughts, as opposed to the Other Side, which is the repository of positive and helpful notions and fresh ideas. Thoughts in the lower two levels become muddy and confusing, like putting too many colors together. So these thoughts are the discarded trash, and the lower two levels become the dumping ground for the "nuclear fallout" of our minds. Some of that gets really ugly.

So the lower two levels are essentially mental mind dumps. Sometimes I think they leak back and forth among themselves, but they don't ever get up past the fifth level because that's Lilith's domain. Insanity and religious fanaticism dip in to these nightmarish levels. The biggest fanatics can be the people who are always preaching about hellfire and brimstone. Thoughts become things, so they begin to create their own demons. They bring these awful, ugly, horrible things into their minds. So what they end up doing is possessing themselves with their own thoughts.

Q: Are the thoughts in the lower two levels mostly unusable creations?

A. Yes. Most of them come from the dream world or from the realm of insanity, which has a tendency to be able to open those lower levels. The insane usually don't come and get such thoughts, but they do seem to hallucinate them up. Eliciting the two levels of nightmare-quality thoughts isn't important, except for the simple fact that you know they exist and that they remain on their specified level. They're not really made up of any reality, as the first four levels are.

As opposed to the first four levels, the bottom two are made of "thought-things." In other words, they're creations of humankind, while Lilith and all the high-level entities are actual creations of God. It goes to show you that human beings, although great and part of God, don't create many good things. The only way that evil thoughts and creations escape from the underworld is through thought processes, and even then they're transparently reflected, like a vision might come to those who are mentally ill. In other words, they're not really there—they're actually brought through via hallucinations.

What I'm trying to say is that no ugly creature from the lower two levels is going to come and bite your leg tonight. Remember: *There is no such thing.*

❦

PART II

THE SEVEN LEVELS
OF LIFE ON EARTH

Introduction to Part II

It's interesting to note that, just as there are seven levels of the underworld, there are also seven levels of life on Earth. I remember when I was in Egypt and went to the Great Pyramid of Cheops—as I was ascending the Grand Gallery, which is not an easy climb, I began to envision pictures of humankind's progression through life on the walls. (You see, the Great Pyramid was never meant to just be a burial chamber; rather, it was intended to be a temple showing humans' rise into the peace and glory of the afterlife.)

So it is that we have stages we must go through in this life. I don't just mean the physical or hormonal changes we endure—although I'll touch on those as well—but the levels that our soul reaches to survive and progress for our own learning and spiritual advancement. The deeper we go into creation and our own part in it, the more we become aware that everything great and small has order and purpose. And those who claim that there's no order just have to look around and see that none of this could be (or is) coincidental. . . .

CHAPTER 3

THE FIRST LEVEL—BIRTH

The first thing that happens when our soul enters the physical body is that we start on one of the hardest, strength-building journeys we ever experience.

After doing so many regressions, I've stopped taking individuals under hypnosis completely through the birth process, since making my clients relive its agonies doesn't really serve any purpose. I touch on it and then put them in the observant position, which means that they can see their birth, but they don't have to experience it. They can have the knowledge that it's very painful to be born into this living hell and be separated from our bliss and all our loved ones without having to go through it.

Even though we're never alone here on Earth, it's not like being Home. Here we change from a spiritual, glorified body that has no illness or worries to one that's gravity bound. Some of our souls stay in the uterus a short time, but more often we enter just before birth. That's because, as Francine says, it's too boring for the entity to just sit inside the mother with nothing to do.

Many studies have tried to prove that trauma that happens to a mother during pregnancy affects her baby, but I've seen from experience that the entity makes its own chart and knows what it's chosen. Sometimes it will retract because it feels that it picked too much; then there are the cases in which an entity leaves early, possibly to help the parents learn a lesson from loss (which they'd also put in their own charts). Nothing is by accident, and as difficult as it is for anyone to lose a baby, we must remember that it was planned by those involved or was, at the very least, an option to happen. Parents blame themselves many times for their child's death, but they shouldn't—unless they were abusing themselves by taking drugs, drinking, or doing all the wrong things. Even then, the entity coming in would know that and could have retracted to try to make the mother or father come to his or her senses.

Babies in the uterus *do* seem to do better when the mother is more serene, perhaps because she listens to soft music, meditates, or even reads aloud. For you expectant mothers out there, remember that you're carrying a real knowing entity inside of you, which is only separated from this world by a thin membrane of skin.

I'm sure that the reason my oldest son, Paul, was so fearful when he was a baby was because I was in such an abusive marriage. My little guy didn't want to be one foot away from me—he didn't sleep, but what was more important was that he was so afraid. He grew out of it to be very strong, but that first year was tough . . . and on top of it, I was one of those mothers who had the postpartum blues (except they didn't know anything about it in those days). Yet by the time my youngest son, Chris, came along, I'd learned to try to ignore my situation and separate myself—as a consequence, he came in quieter and slept more.

I've always said to be careful what you say around an infant. There's a real entity in there with a mind and previous lives, and it can be imprinted instantly (as regressionists and psychiatrists can attest to because they've unearthed birth traumas).

Imagine coming into life: You're traveling down a narrow tunnel, your air is half-squeezed out of your lungs, you're roughly pulled out, and if you're not smacked, you still have large hands grabbing you, bright lights glaring in your face, and strangers milling around you. You're also naked and cold; people are putting things in your nose, eyes, and mouth; and you're small and vulnerable—you've just left the haven of Home, loved ones, and peace and happiness. No wonder babies cry!

Now all your organs have to work, whereas they didn't need to on the Other Side. Even though you were in a glorified, tangible body when you were Home, you didn't have to worry about breathing, pumping blood through your heart, or eliminating waste. You now have to sleep, eat, and get accustomed to seeing, hearing, and feeling in a world that's a hundred times more dense than where you came from.

Well-meaning people make funny faces, talk in strange and loud voices with sounds that nobody can understand (including a baby!), and give you "tummy raspberries" and plenty of hugs whenever they come in contact with you. Imagine yourself as an entity who's just come into life and has to endure these loving but sometimes ridiculous displays of affection—how could you not be confused? After all, you just came from a place where conversations *can* be verbal, but most of the communication is through real and valid telepathy. And as a final insult, in your soul's passive memory you probably know what you're in for in this life. In fact, you'll probably retain vivid recollections of your Home and other lives until about the age of three, at which point they'll fade.

So many mothers and fathers have told me that their little ones saw and spoke with their "imaginary playmates" (which are actually their spirit guides) and even loved ones who have passed over. Children should be listened to, not discouraged, when they tell us stories of their "other family," where they lived before, or even whom they see and what they said. On the other hand, they shouldn't be pestered to tell us these stories either . . . we should let them come naturally.

My own grandson Willy, who was born after my dad's death, found a picture of him in my drawer. He then turned to his own father (my psychic son, Chris) and me and said, "Look, here's Old Poppy." "Old Poppy" was what we called my father later on in his life! Then Willy got a strange look on his face, and in a deeper voice than usual said, "That's my girl"—which was my father's favorite thing to say to me—while gazing directly at me. He then went on with his baby gibberish, as my son and I sat stunned. I had chills all over my body as I realized that my father had been able to get through Willy's pliable and innocent mind for a moment to send me a message.

Similarly, when Paul was two years old, he told me that he'd lived in France with a mother and father who ran a vineyard; while at about the same age, Chris told me that he was a cowboy who got shot, he had a horse named Cinder, and his daughter ran out of the house and held his head when he was dying. Now you can say that my boys saw these things on television, but no two-year-old uses the words *daughter* or *vineyard*.

Memory has to fade, because if it didn't, we wouldn't make it through life on this planet. Even though I'm convinced that we always suffer with a type of homesickness that's in our spiritual DNA, if we could actually recall the bliss and happiness of the Other Side in detail, we'd all be jumping off bridges, saying, "To hell with this Earth life!"

CHAPTER 4

THE SECOND LEVEL— THE FORMATIVE YEARS

Thanks to 18 years of teaching, half of which were spent in elementary schools, I saw the early formative years firsthand. This is where not only cell memory from past lives comes in, but also when our vision of ourselves takes hold. The memory of the Other Side has faded, and we start on the difficult trek of learning and fulfilling our own written chart. We begin to learn to walk and navigate a body that's heavy and gravity bound. It seems a little strange to say, but it's almost like someone who's had a stroke having to learn everything all over again.

During this time in a perfect world—which this clearly is not— we'd be cuddled and loved, fed, kept warm, played with, and be potty-trained. (I'm not saying that this can't be the norm, but your childhood may be more like mine was, where my grandmother and father gave me love, but none came from my own mother.)

So much of this level also relates to how the world reacts to us and we react to it. This is also where night terrors or regressive or aggressive behavior can start, and our likes and dislikes and even our loves start forming. In other words, we become aware of who we are and what we really enjoy (and *don't* enjoy).

Many times we're forced into sports or piano lessons, not because we want them, but because our parents feel that they're doing us an injustice if they don't offer us enough activities. On the other side of the coin, some caregivers feel that supplying food, clothing, and shelter and simply fulfilling physical needs is enough. Nevertheless, you can't be too hard on parents at any age and time, as they're always doing the best they can. For example, I was born during the Depression, so just to survive was a feat.

But then we have people who can be so affluent from an early age and whose parents find it easier to buy than to talk and love. Regardless (and I'll probably say this many times), we pick all these situations to form what we'll become: Some grow from being fed from the proverbial silver spoon to becoming great humanitarians or leaders, while others who are given the golden opportunities of wealth and education spiral down into drugs and self-abuse. It's the same as some individuals rising above an environment of poverty, drugs, alcohol, broken homes, discrimination, and the like to make something of themselves; while others sink deeper into the mire of overblown ego, self-depravation, or crime. The soul begins to meet its challenges at this point . . . gradually and often painfully.

Speaking of challenges, school can be a big one, because we're separated from the known and possibly stable environment of our home and placed in an alien place with people who reflect us favorably or unfavorably. Are we too tall, too fat, too short, or too thin? Are we part of the "in crowd" or are we a nerd or rejected? This is when outward discipline doesn't seem to fit with what's inside of us. Unfortunately, this is also where games are played on us or we learn from them to do what we feel we must do to survive, such as whom to play up to, whom to ignore, or even who will love us for us (which is a lifelong challenge).

We "cut our teeth" both at home and as a result of the peer pressure around us. Our siblings (if we have any) and parents play a big part in our spiritual and social development. We wonder, *Do my brothers and sisters love me?* and *Do my parents favor one of us over the other?* Such questions loom large and get ever bigger in the development of our soul in the years to come.

❧ ❧

Now before we go any further, let's explore our spiritual development. With some of us it kicks in right away, but most of the time it takes a lot of life experience—including role-playing, lying, protecting ourselves, or self-deception—before we hit the core of what we incarnated for. Many times life is like a war, and just as a soldier may not dwell on the things he has to do because of the situation he's in, our need to both survive and be loved can often lead us down a road that we wouldn't normally take. Here again, the chart that's always present kicks in, pushing us to continually learn and perfect.

Obstacles are just a part of life. For example, I knew that my mother didn't like me, and the fact that my father loved me so much didn't help (because of her jealousy). Well, I could have gone two ways with this—I could have become like the person who persecuted me, or I could have become a better person and parent because of it. Each of us can be punished or have jealousy around us just because we are who we are—not because we've done anything wrong or bad—and this is the most confusing thing for the soul to understand.

Every one of us inherently wants to be loved and have some attention paid to us. Unfortunately, we learn that crying, begging, cajoling, throwing fits, manipulating, and controlling don't work very well. No one has elected us king or queen, and even if they had, such a position has its own troubles. (Even some of my very wealthy and powerful clients have problems you can't imagine. They worry, *Will I lose my wealth? Do people love me for me?*)

We also get to the point that we realize it's just a tough world out there. We learn our likes and dislikes, and we'll always run into competition with others to get ahead—but will we sacrifice our principles, ethics, and spirituality to beat them? Whether it's as simple as potty-training, playing, being punished, or even getting away with actions that we should be held accountable for, on this second level we're going to find out who our friends and enemies are. Hopefully, we'll embrace what the actions of others teach us and become better people for it.

CHAPTER 5

THE THIRD LEVEL— LEARNING

As we start to leave our formative years, all that we've experienced thus far begins to take hold. It may be slow at first, but whether it's in our consciousness or not, we begin to gradually realize that what we put out comes back—even if it's as simple as if we're mean, no one will want to be with us.

Even in school, learning is very minimal at the beginning and takes a backseat to the activating facets of peer pressure. School becomes a microcosm of life, as we ask ourselves, *Do I like it or do I hate it? Can I make friends? Can I learn to be a friend myself?* Here's where we begin to see the bullies, the manipulators, and the ones who are favored or picked on—sometimes just because they're different.

We also begin to not only have awareness of our peers, but of our teachers as well. Hopefully we already have a great deal of innate knowledge, but every time and era has its own sets of morals and ethics. Women in Africa can walk around bare-breasted, for instance, but here it wouldn't be morally or socially correct. To be a courtesan in France in the 1700s was acceptable (and such an individual would even have held a fairly high social status), but in the 21st century, this activity would label one a "whore" or an "adulteress." I'm not criticizing or condoning either—I'm just showing you how different the outlook on morals can be due to culture and how the mores of society often change over the years.

At this point, the Other Side begins to rear its head, but not as much as adolescence and the idea of love start to operate in our soul minds. We begin to love our parents, and know that we do. We pick our friends and negate others. *Am I loved?* is a theme that runs through all the levels, yet so many times this sets us up to reject or be rejected. Most of us can be fooled at one time or another, but we do gradually learn to discern who among us is kind or hateful . . . even if they happen to be within our own family.

❧❧

The third level is when we start to have a religious belief or at least a curiosity about God. For example, my grandchildren began to ask about God and the Other Side when they were on this level, even though they hadn't been exposed to any dogma. And when I was teaching school (long before I ever started religious instruction), young people would wonder where they came from. Yes, they can be curious about how babies are made, but more than that, they genuinely want to understand their origins. This stems directly from their charts.

Here we also begin to learn guilt, and we develop a conscience. Of course we know right from wrong, but it helps if our chart has been written definitively enough. Not that we don't write every nuance into it, but Francine says that sometimes we get remiss and feel that we'll just automatically know what we do on the Other Side. Therefore, it can take us a little longer to get into our morals, conscience, and spiritual awareness. (We eventually come around, but it's better to do so earlier rather than later.) As we grow, our spirituality should grow with us. I'm convinced that as we progress through the levels, we all eventually begin to feel what's right for us, whether it's organized religion or just eternal seeking. It's amazing to see that the more advanced we become, the more we search for truth, knowledge, and answers, just as Jesus said to.

This level is where we discover our preferences and so-called roles in the world around us—this includes who the bullies or baddies are, and even that boys and girls aren't alike. Whereas before we didn't see color or ethnic distinctions, now we begin to notice that we are in fact different from other races and creeds. If we carry enough spirituality and aren't programmed otherwise, then as we grow up and mature, such differences won't matter. That's because in our spirit mind, we'll come to the knowledge that we've all been everything in our past lives.

Our subconscious knows that in all probability we've been every color, creed, and race, and have lived lives as both male and female. (Although if we're created as either a male or female, we stay the sex we were created as on the Other Side. We may come into a life on Earth as the opposite sex for the experience—that is, to learn—and this is one of the main reasons for homosexuality.) Eventually we begin to have a sense of knowing that everything is accepted by our loving and all-forgiving God.

Now we also become aware of what we can possibly excel at. We realize that we're better at some things than others—maybe we can't be an artist or a sports star, but we have a talent for math and chemistry or vice versa. And throughout the entire process, we follow our chart and excel.

This is probably the hardest level of life because it's the one of active learning and extends for such a long period of time—from our formative years into full adulthood. In fact, it doesn't really stop until we die . . . but it certainly helps fulfill our mission for God.

CHAPTER 6

THE FOURTH LEVEL—
PREADOLESCENCE AND
PUBERTY

This next level is when life really kicks in, and I mean it can give us a hard jolt in the backside. We may have understood peer pressure before, but not as profoundly as we do now. We're no longer in the so-called womb of the home, nor are we even in the safe haven of grammar school in which we were with the people we grew up with, and we learned to survive. No, now we're suddenly thrown in to a new environment—and on top of that, our classmates have split up and we're faced with different teachers, friends, and routines. It's a type of culture shock, and our human side wants to please and be accepted as never before. A professor I dearly loved and admired once said that these years of preadolescence and puberty make up the vision of ourselves that we carry for most of our lives. Regardless, we do mature beyond this level.

This is the time of facing tremendous peer pressure to smoke or drink, plus the fatal attraction of drugs is seemingly everywhere. In fact, I remember being on a TV show called *People Are Talking* almost 30 years ago, and someone asked me what the worst thing our young people had to fear was. When I replied, "Drugs," everyone got quiet and hushed over it. Sure, we had illegal substances back in my day, but not like now. For most of us, Coke meant a soft drink, and the worst thing we had to contend with was alcohol. (Fortunately, as an aside, I can't handle any of it. I get violently ill when I drink alcohol, and I'm so sensitive to drugs that I have a hard time even taking antibiotics or any type of painkillers. I had a doctor once say, "I hope you don't ever get seriously ill because you're allergic to everything." Isn't that a pleasant thought?)

Even if we happen to get caught up in substance abuse, spirituality usually does kick in, helping us realize that we can't numb ourselves to life. If we go off track, getting back on is imperative, as it means that we've learned. If we *haven't* learned, we might very well go back Home and choose to return in another life to rectify what we didn't complete in this one (or any in which we didn't face life head-on). We must remember that no substance can take away life's tragedies or disappointments because we always have to come down and face them eventually. It we take drugs to get up, go to bed, or get through the day, we become like a robot trying to smother pain, grief, or disappointment—which are all the things we learn from. We simply can't perfect in a state of anesthesia.

On this level we also encounter gangs, which spring up because they seem exciting. Also, preadolescence and puberty bring with them a feeling of *Nothing can harm me . . . I'm impervious to danger.* In addition, so many young people feel that there's nothing to look forward to, especially when they see the world in chaos. With the family unit breaking down, kids looking for acceptance find it in a different type of family unit. The head of the gang is like the father figure, and the rest are like brothers and sisters who stick together against the adversity of the world. They even call each other "Bro" or "Homie," which is short for "brother" or "one of the family."

Now most parents don't intend for their family to fall apart—most of the time they're so busy working and trying to get ahead that they forget how to gather their loved ones around and really talk to them. If family members could all just sit down to dinner together and ask each other what happened that was good or bad during the day and really listen to each other, this would accomplish two things: (1) It would make each person feel important, and (2) it would also help everyone in the family understand where their joys and worries are. The lines of communication would then be open.

I know that communicating with kids in this age group is never easy because of the hormonal changes that are occurring—most of the time the young people in question don't even know what their own bodies are doing. As my 13-year-old granddaughter told me the other night, "Bagdah [her name for me], sometimes I just cry for no reason at all."

I replied, "Oh, Angelia, when I was your age, I'd go in my room and write poetry, listen to sad songs, and cry . . . and then someone would call, and I'd go see my friends, and we'd suddenly be laughing and having fun."

She just stared at me and asked, "Really? You did that, too?"

"Yes, honey," I answered, smothering a smile. "Bagdah was once your age, believe it or not." And that's another thing: Don't ever let yourself forget how hard it was to be young. The old cliché of "Well, when I was your age, I had to do such and such . . ." doesn't hold any water. It's much better to sympathize and listen. After all, everyone wants to either find someone good to look up to or be the person whom others can look up to. My Grandma Ada was 70 when I was born, but she was a wonderful role model— and so were some of the nuns and priests I knew, as well as my father, who always listened to me. It's never too early to talk to your children about pedophiles, drugs, alcohol, and smoking. My grandmother used to say that if someone can ask a question, then he or she is ready to learn.

Some kids on this level may resort to stealing or indulging in other illegal activity. After all, our society seems to actually endorse a life of crime—from fancy cars to loose and beautiful women and plenty of money to spend—the entertainment industry has certainly glamorized it enough. Nevertheless, every culture, no matter how primitive, has its laws and morals. In fact, the first prerequisite of human behavior seems to be that everyone has to follow the rules of the country, city, province, or tribe; otherwise, chaos erupts. Unfortunately, there aren't many idols out there for kids to look up to these days—yes, some in the public eye tend to do the right thing, but so many others are all about sexuality. Of course you can't really blame them, as society dictates what sells.

Sometimes adolescents feel that bullying their way through life or being disrespectful is "cool." I've always believed that if we adults are respectful to young people, then we'll learn just as much as they will. Some of us may come by this trait naturally, while others will have to learn it—regardless, respect brings respect, and celebrating who we *and* others are always pays off. I saw it in teaching when the principal used to routinely give me the most difficult students to deal with. Making them feel that they had value made such a difference . . . and it works with anyone of any age to know that they matter in the eyes of God, and it raises their spirituality and self-esteem.

⊱⊰

While many of the challenges of adolescence are obvious in nature, many of them can also come from past-life bleed-throughs. I've watched the girls in Angelia's class, and I recall the kids from my own teaching experiences: Some of them start fussing with their hair more and get more involved in clothes, music, and makeup, whereas others stay "little girls" a bit longer. As minimal as this may seem, it can actually be a past-life recall to get older faster or even develop phobias about certain incidents such as fire, drowning, loss, or abandonment.

To digress, this can also happen at an early age with night terrors—which parents can cure by going in and telling the sleeping child that the issue at hand is in the past. Just as very young children remember past lives before their memory begins to fade, carried-over fears really start to surface in puberty. For example, a girl I once taught in the sixth grade couldn't even entertain the idea of having kids because she was afraid that she'd die. This was because in an earlier life, she'd died in childbirth at an early age.

We can rid ourselves of such fears by asking God to remove and absorb negativity *from any life* right before we go to bed, and we can do this for ourselves at any age. It's like we've experienced it and no longer need the "morphic resonance" to haunt us in this life. Morphic remembrance means that we've carried past-life memories over, both good and bad. This explains why we have phobias, illness, and even depression; yet we can also bring over marvelous talents such as musical or artistic ability, writing talent, or even a predisposition for making money—wonderful things that are lodged in our passive memory.

I was watching TV the other night and happened to catch Whoopi Goldberg in a documentary about her life. I've always admired her and her integrity, but this time I noticed her saying something very significant. She stated that from the time she was a small child, all she ever wanted to do was be an entertainer: an actress and comedian. She said she didn't know where this desire came from, but it was always what she wanted to be. *I* know where it came from . . . Whoopi used to perform in plays in England and France in lives before this one—so of course she'd come in with this great cell memory of having been an entertainer before. So regardless of whether it's from your chart or past-life tendencies, if you keep the center of your soul clear and clean, you'll find your passion.

Many times people say, "I always wanted to be a doctor [or lawyer or what have you], but I became an engineer instead." Well, you were supposed to . . . it was written in your chart! You may have a desire to be on Broadway because you have a bleed-through from a past life in which you were a dancer or singer. In other words, what you've previously done comes back as a yearning, in the same way that phobias and fears can affect you. On the other side of the coin, you may be a savant about music in this life because you were so good at it in past ones that it carried over and you excel at it now. Look at Mozart, who was playing and composing at the age of four. That didn't come from just one life—he wanted to come down and finish what he'd started in a past one.

Your chart will kick in, and if you deviate, that doesn't mean you're off track; it just means that you're experiencing what you wrote. But as I stated earlier, you can't let the world steer you away for too long or you will suffer a soul's yearning. It's true that we all have a real homesickness for the Other Side, but what I'm talking about here is that deep, hollow nothingness that goes beyond depression. But no matter how bad it gets, you can't bail out of this life because if you do, you'll just have to come back and do it all over again. Religion has always said that if you commit suicide, you go to hell. Well, that's true—you'll come back to Earth, which is the only hell there is.

Sure, life can be a party sometimes, but it was never meant to be one big, continually happy shindig. If it were, we'd never learn. We may think that we're confused, but if we're diligent, our chart will kick in and hold firm. Good looks or bad, college or no college, prom queen or not, we picked it all—the rub comes in what we do with it.

❧ ❧

Getting back to the fourth level, an obvious interest in the opposite sex really begins to develop here, and it's the beginning of crushes (and rejection, too). Puppy love is nothing to make fun of, as it can be a very painful process—but it can also be a definite learning experience to help us recognize the true feelings that will hopefully come in time. That is, it gets us ready to differentiate between permanent love and more transient emotions.

Sex also comes into play here. At the risk of sounding like an evangelist, sex is wonderful but promiscuity is never, ever an option. It not only makes you feel used, but you can also become jaded when the real thing comes along. I'm not criticizing or condoning sexual activity, but this is another thing that's quite different now than it was in my day, as we have the terrible and unstoppable threat of STDs (sexually transmitted diseases), HIV, and AIDS. I've even heard young people say after they contracted HIV, "Well, the person I got it from looked clean" . . . as if such afflictions would be written on the individual's forehead. Yet like anything else, if you've charted promiscuity or to contract a serious illness, that doesn't necessarily mean that you've gone off track. Maybe you have, but you can also turn a negative experience into a good example for everyone else.

And for God's sake (literally), let's not fall into the trap of saying that all the gay people who contracted AIDS were off track, or it was God's will to punish them. (Christ never condemned gays; he only hated hypocrites. Look at religion and some of its dogma and then go back to the New Testament to see if you can find Christ's words supporting any form of prejudice.) Francine has said that as a general rule, gay people picked that lifestyle to show others not to be prejudicial.

Don't jump to the conclusion that every illness we get is punishment for some sort of wrongdoing on our part—more times than not, we chose it to help ourselves and others learn and move up spiritually. We should also be judicious in all the pleasures we have. To some people, life is a candy store, and they feel that they can take their fill without getting sick. Well, I'm here to tell you that it's easier to stay on track if you do *everything* in moderation.

If we're not diligent, we begin to develop real stress on the fourth level. Don't ever delude yourself that you didn't have any tension when you were younger—adolescents not only pick it up from the news and their teachers and parents, but their tomorrows are more uncertain than they've ever been. (Even people that I see in other countries don't have the pressures we have, as they truly have a live-for-the-day philosophy. But then again, we do pick what country, what birthday, what parents, and even what stressors we're going to endure to expand our soul.)

Adolescence can bring with it the fear of not only being left out, but also low self-esteem; or, on the other hand, too much ego or a false sense of self. Sometimes this is when we begin to put on a mask to hide our insecurities. I've noticed that much of what teenagers face today is a type of fatalism, like a sense of "What's the use? The world is in such a state it probably won't be here for long anyway." So many take the attitude to just live it up for now. This is different from adopting the motto of "one day at a time"—it's almost a panicked need to complete everything and do it in a hurry before it all goes away.

Of course things now *are* better than they were in the "good old days"—after all, young people used to get married so early that I'm sure they didn't even have time for puberty. The reason for this that was since everyone died so early, they had to get busy and get married and procreate. Now kids have millions of choices, which is great, but sometimes that has its drawbacks in that they don't know which way to go because of peer pressure and so many options, along with parental pressure to succeed.

Lots of people have asked me to write a book about teenagers, but for now I hope that this chapter has given you some insight into this critical developmental stage . . . whether you're a teenager yourself or are raising one.

৩৩৩ ৩৩৩

CHAPTER 7

THE FIFTH LEVEL—
YOUNG ADULTHOOD

Now we really begin to gear up into what we're going to do with our lives. What career choice are we going to make? Should we go to college, or do we just feel better plying a trade? Because of our choices, many of us start one thing and then end up with another. I was always a psychic, for instance, but I also taught school and then started a foundation. (True, it was still teaching, but on a higher level.) Then, at the age of 50, I wrote my first book.

I smile when I hear people say that it's too late to start something—it's *never* too late to follow what you charted to do . . . in fact, it's better to do it late than to let it fall into nothingness. Even if you just try, there are what we might call "points" for that. After all, everything in the universe is tied tightly together, and every action has a reaction, so who's to say that what you start, someone else won't pick up and finish? It's something like a relay race: You pass the baton to the next person, or you at least leave an imprint, no matter how small, on somebody else's life. Yes, you charted this, but it's how you deal with it that makes your soul strong. You're going to go through tough times no matter what, so why not do so with some grace and the realization that you picked it *and* you have strength of character in the process?

If we go away to college, the cocoon of the same people we're used to being with is disrupted, and being away from home can be traumatic. Regardless of what people say, most of us don't take to change as a general rule. Sure, some acclimate easier, but we all become disrupted in some way. (Even vacations can affect us in this way at times—we look forward to getting away, and then we work so hard at "having fun" that we have to come home to relax.)

While at school, we wonder: *What should I major in? Do I like my professors? Do I fit in? What about friends? Are my grades good enough?* This can be one of the most stressful times of our lives, as we now have to view ourselves as a singular unit that has to make its way in the world without the sanctity of home, friends, and family. We're on a journey to find our niche in life, to make money to survive, and to perhaps even provide for a family.

For us women, it's not like in times past where we were just supposed to get married and have children—females now aspire to have careers just like men and often get an education for that purpose, or at least to learn and better themselves. Even when I was going to college, it was only acceptable for a woman to become a nurse or teacher, not the CEO of a company, like many are today. Now things are wide open for women. While there's still some discrimination (God knows I can attest to that!), at least we have a better chance than our Victorian-era sisters did. For that matter, even in the 1950s, women couldn't progress like we can now.

I have to admit that men can have it harder in a different way. Society grades males by what they do in life, the cars they drive, how much money they make, and how they provide for their families. Now there's nothing wrong with material gain, but when it begins to rule you, then that becomes your god, and spirituality suffers. God or your chart (unless you've deemed otherwise) doesn't expect you not to have nice things or enjoy life—if that were true, it wouldn't be here for you to aim for. It's only when it becomes an addiction that problems arise . . . and make no mistake, material gain and acquiring more and more things *can* be an addiction, just like any other obsessive behavior, in that it affects your spirituality in a negative way.

When this happens, you need to sit down and wonder what you're making up for or rewarding yourself for. Is it insecurity? A lack of self-esteem? Ego satisfaction? It's a known and unaddressed fact that material possessions will only make you happy for a short time, and then it's on to the next thing and the next, until it can never be enough. As the old cliché goes, you're not going to be on your deathbed wishing that you'd driven your Mercedes or Bentley more. It's your actions in life—what you give and do in loving and helping—that you take with you. Many cynics will say a man's accomplishments can be measured by the material things he's garnered . . . I say, see how many people attend his funeral.

Some on the fourth level can fall into the "easy-money" pit . . . by that, I mean criminal activity. There comes a time when wealth and passion can come together or be in opposition. What's life worth if there's no joy but just "things"? We can become so stressed that we become like a hamster on a wheel, just trying to get ahead. Well, the illegal way is *never* the answer. We've seen this in both petty criminal activity and in the questionable actions of large corporations and even governments. Everyone suffers from such behavior, as we all have a moral obligation to live by right actions—once trust has been broken, it's almost impossible to get back.

Even if we try to justify our illegal behavior, karma will assert and enact itself. Whether or not we see it right away, it *will* activate, for that's the law of the universe. Francine said an interesting thing to me the other day. She said that because Earth's schematic is changing (she didn't say *ending*), if you just sit back and wait, in about five years you'll see karma come to the person who's done something with an impure motive.

But please remember that vengeance creates cause and effect. Many times in our minds we wish that the person who hurt us will "get it" and can even fantasize about how that will happen, but that's only in our mind and it's a human emotion. Sometimes it's the only way we have to get over our own hurt, but we don't act on it.

Some of us may go so far as to wish that the offending party die, but that still doesn't cause death. If that were the case, no tyrant would have lasted very long thanks to all the hate that was directed his way. Sometimes clients who have gone through a bitter divorce tell me that death would have been easier to deal with than the pain of rejection. This could be because death is natural and we know that our loved one is safe on the Other Side, but if you're left for another person, the pain can be soul-deep.

I know this from firsthand experience with my third husband. Out of the blue he decided to leave me, and in a week he was gone. I had some great scenarios of what I wanted to have happen to him, but that soon gave way to relief, especially when I began to hear from loved ones how cruel he'd been. It was a learning experience about trust—and then deception and greed—but when the pain subsided, life got so much better.

You'd think that these types of lessons would be carried with you from lifetime to lifetime (and some people actually do carry them over, as is evinced by their spirituality), but think of how much it takes you to learn something even now. It's all trial and error, and each life has a different scenario. It's like a play in that you're given lines to read, but the plot is different every time. So no matter where you are or what career you're in as a young adult, what will ultimately carry you through are the values you embrace and the priorities you form.

⤬⤬⤬

Young adulthood is another time when we begin to make friends, even though many of us still keep our old pals. (Here again, we're never too old to make friends; that is, if *we* are friends.) Jobs set up fresh environments in which we can meet and befriend new people.

We realize that it can be a tough world out there, and one of the first things we'll run in to is whether or not we like our job or career. We have to learn to get along with co-workers (which is peer pressure again), and we can perform with zest or be sluggish and lazy. Usually unhappiness and malaise is a sign that we're in the wrong place, but programmed security often keeps us stuck in a miserable working environment full of politics and backbiting. It's better to take less and live more frugally than to suffer such stress in the pursuit of the "almighty dollar."

Now we talk about goals a lot, but through all of life and its relationships, happiness, disappointments, family, and so forth, we find out how our goals measure up to our spiritual potential. All the rest falls by the wayside if our soul isn't fulfilled. How does that come about? Well, it simply boils down to one of the best rules there is: "Do unto others as you would have them do unto you." Or, like I've said so many times: "Love God, do good, and then shut up and go Home."

As we get into adulthood, we should seek and read, and then we'll be aware that life isn't easy, but without dogma it's much easier. The more spiritual we become, the more we'll be able to discern who's good for us and who isn't. We need the negative to bounce off of and learn from, but we don't have to spend our life cultivating it.

This is the level in which you'll usually decide to get married or just enjoy the single life. You can go through many experiences in much stronger relationships than you had as adolescents, because most entities are programmed to couple and procreate. (The ones who don't shouldn't be looked down upon, as they've usually made this choice because they had many children in a past life.) If your chart says marry, you will; if not, you won't. Even picking the wrong mate is in your chart for you to learn from. If you do divorce and you have kids, then for God's sake be friends for the children (that is, if it's possible and the other party isn't abusive). But just because you think that you can do better when things with your mate hit a boring patch, you'll find that the grass isn't greener on the other side of the fence . . . it's burnt. How many times have we seen a person get a divorce and then remarry someone who might be a different size or shape than their previous spouse was, but is the exact same type of person inside? This just proves that you're going to learn your lessons, one way or the other.

We also have to be vigilant that we don't just talk spirituality, but *activate* on it. For example, I know a man who owns a whole area of California. He raised his own children; then, when his brother got into trouble, he took in all four of *his* children. Out of love and spiritual essence, he's raising his brother's children plus taking care of his own aging parents. So regardless of what this man has, he's following not only *his* chart, but the universal one mandating that we take care of each other.

Some adults choose to live with their parents. Perhaps it's an only child, or even one of many, who wants to stay and be the caregiver. Some might think that this would be a lonely life, but I've asked some of my clients who have done this and they feel very gratified, even to the point that they were so thankful to be by their parents' bedside as they passed. I had my own family, but I also took care of my parents until they died—and I wouldn't have changed a minute of it, even though at times it was exhausting. It's not because I'm saying "Aren't I great," but we in the U.S. should do what many cultures do: Revere their elders and take care of them. Now if the elderly people are a danger to themselves, then outside help is definitely needed, but I'm talking here about all the folks my ministers and I have seen in nursing homes who are forgotten and abandoned by their families.

Some individuals, however, are loners and like living in remote places—and some even choose the homeless life. You might pity them, but I've seen more people who live what we might call a poor and singular life be happy than so many of us on the financial merry-go-round are. The homeless seem to really care for each other and enjoy a culture unto themselves. You could try to bring them into society, but the next thing you know, they'd be back on the streets. It's similar to some people who are incarcerated—it's all they know, so they feel secure with their lifestyle. That doesn't mean that we shouldn't give food and help to the indigent, but a person has to want to change his or her life before he or she will listen to anyone else.

As I've said many times, who are we to judge others' charts or how they choose to live? After all, we certainly don't know what they did in a past life that made them want this experience. Now don't feel that if your life is hard that you've been a bad person in a past life—on the contrary, you've chosen to live through everything . . . the good, the bad, *and* the ugly.

Life is so full of questions that it gives me comfort to know that no matter how many choices we think we have, we'll still end up with our preordained chart. As corny as it sounds, everything does turn out for the best, even if we don't think so at the time. Without the tragedies we must face, our lives would never take those turns that bring us closer to our own spiritual center.

❦

CHAPTER 8

THE SIXTH LEVEL— ADULTHOOD

Young adulthood and adulthood blend into each other just as adulthood and old age do. In fact, we find that many of the levels of Earthly life merge together before they become more defined and singular. Several of the traits and problems that would seem to be indigenous to a certain level can also be carried over to another level . . . that's just life as we know it to be.

So, in adulthood, we have our careers and relationships; and we begin to get into insurance, credit, the IRS, buying a house, and the inevitable bills, too. This level also tends to be where we start raising a family. We used to just do the best we could by talking to our kids; disciplining them; praising them; spiritually teaching them; and, of course, providing food, clothing, and shelter. Now we have thousands of books to tell us what to do and what not to do, or what we shouldn't have done and how we can rectify it. Not that this is wrong . . . but if we're caring, loving parents and become role models, that's the end of it.

We also now have all these learning disorders. I'm not saying that children can't be dyslexic or are sometimes slower to learn than their peers are, but we label everyone too quickly these days. When I was in school myself and then taught for 18 years, I saw the "slow" ones, the "bright" ones, the "dreamers," and the "savants," and you just reach each one in a different way. (I'm proud to say that I still see my first class of third graders when I go back to Kansas City, Missouri, and 98 percent of them made it just fine.)

If you give a child a label, they're branded and have to work off of that stigma. For example, I got an e-mail from a young boy of 12 some years back who said that he was stupid because he had attention deficit disorder (ADD). I wrote him back and said, "No way—you'll strongly get into music." He replied that all he loved was music. He sent me his first CD about a month ago.

Some kids need to be challenged in a certain subject. Not everyone is going to like math, for instance . . . God knows I didn't. I was more interested in theology, English, and art. I even helped my boyfriend at the time with Latin, while he tried to tutor me in math. Not only could I not understand it, I didn't want to—it just made no sense to me. I told my teacher that I'd never use algebra in my life. Her response was, "Yes, you will." Well, guess what? At almost 70 years of age, I've never used algebra in any form.

So my chart led me into teaching, spirituality, the psychic arts, and writing. Could I have tried to do something else for a time? Of course, but my chart would have kicked me back on the course I'd already written for myself. The one thing that I should explain in greater detail is that no matter what path you take, your chart will win out. (It also bears mentioning here that Mother God can intercept your chart, for She is the miracle worker. I'm sure that miracles can be preordained to a certain extent without disturbing the ripple of destiny, but She is known as the Great Interceptor. Most of my study groups, congregations, and ministers pray to God, angels, and even our loved ones; but when we need something in particular, we petition Her. This just shows that there can be lateral movement in our charts without interrupting the major tapestry of our life.)

Sometimes I believe that on the Other Side we "bite off more than we can chew," as the old saying goes. It seems that when we're Home, we're in such a state of bliss that we simply pick more than we can handle on Earth. Even though our guides and the Council (advanced entities on the Other Side who advise us) may try to dissuade us, my spirit guide Francine says that more times than not, we feel that we know better . . . only to yell uncle when we get here. It's like being in college, when we come in all gung ho and want to take every course imaginable. Then after the grind, the homework, the professors, the other students, and living conditions set in, we wonder where our mind was! But in order to advance our souls, we have to bite the proverbial bullet and go through it.

So many of you will rightfully ask, "What in the hell was I thinking about? Was I just crazy or drugged to pick all this heartache and pain?" No, you were in full consciousness; after viewing your past lives and making up your chart, you took on this life to perfect. Think about it—if things were easy, where would the learning be, and how would your soul expand? So be good to yourself and realize that you had the courage to come to this hellhole and expand your knowledge.

Francine says that for every negativity that we go through, big or small, our spirit guides can view our souls expanding. We can bitch about it, but we're going to go through it—and that alone will elevate us. Each thing we go through, whether we realize it at the time or not, does make us stronger. It's also really okay to say to God, "Enough is enough," for that won't take away the learning. Like I've said, you can't change your chart, but you *can* shorten or modify it. It's like finishing college in three years instead of four—you still did it, but you were able to give yourself a type of reprieve.

ᨆᨆᨆ

In adulthood we may have picked divorce and single parenthood for ourselves. This is very difficult, as I can tell you from my readings and my own life. Raising two rambunctious boys by myself was really hard, especially when I was working five jobs and doing readings at the same time, but anything was better than being in an abusive marriage. Like most of us, I wanted a family, a home, and a caring husband, but it didn't work out that way. On top of that, when I came to California my parents and sister followed me, and I was the only one working for eight months. Granted, this was in the '60s, but it was still tough until my retired dad got a job selling cars, and my husband finally became a security guard.

You look back and wonder how you managed sometimes, but you wrote these things in your chart, and your choices are to either give up or go forward. I never wanted a divorce—I wanted to be married forever. But I'd love to tell all women in abusive relationships that *nothing* is worth your or your children's health, self-esteem, or welfare; and it's certainly not worth it to stay just for the reason of saying you're married or because of religious dogma.

On the sixth level of life on Earth, we may deal with losing our jobs or staying in careers we hate because we need the economic security. It's different when it's just us, but when we have a family, money can begin to rule our lives. The one outstanding fear that faces this society is being homeless, bankrupt, and (unlike years ago) not being able to rely on the kindness of others. We used to be happy with just scratching out a living, but now we have to "live large." Maybe simpler is better, for if we "buy" our children, they'll later feel that the world owes them and become dependent on "the good life." Truly the happiest people I've seen aren't poor—they have enough and put their families first.

Now I'm not suggesting that we shouldn't reach for the heights so that our minds and hearts can find satisfaction and fulfillment. However, when material things begin to take precedence over what we ought to truly value of ourselves and our loved ones, it becomes a definite problem that leads to financial desperation or the need for wealth. The operative word here is *need*. What do we actually require for survival? The only things that are truly essential in this life are food, clothing, shelter, loved ones, and enough resources to be comfortable. How many cars can we drive? How many clothes or shoes can we wear? How many places can we live in? Understand that I'm not discouraging investments— I'm talking about the obsessive conditioning to have more and more, so we have to *work* more and more, so we keep up with what we don't have time to enjoy anyway!

At this point in life, we begin to worry about how we're going to send our children to college or pay off the student loans that hang over our heads. We're even bombarded by TV commercials advising us to have enough money for funeral arrangements or term insurance so that our families aren't destitute in case something happens. This not only utilizes fear as a driving motive, but it also gives us a nice case of guilt. Of course insurance is a great thing, but not when we can't pay our rent!

Young people these days are worried about retirement and whether Social Security will even be there for them when they come of age. Well, retirement seems repugnant to me. I don't mean the people who retire from one thing to do something else useful—I'm talking about those who just give up, sit on the couch or porch, and read the paper or watch TV all day. This is the easiest way to step right into senility, illness, and death.

Some say that they can't wait to retire so that they can write, paint, sculpt, or travel. These are wonderful pursuits, especially if you've worked at a job you didn't especially care for. By all means, when you retire, immerse yourself in your passion or what you've always wanted to do because if you don't keep your mind active, your body will think you're dead. And if you lie around, your *mind* will think you're dead, sending you into lethargy and depression.

It's also at this time that we begin to worry about our health. Once again, we're bombarded by society's programming: What foods should we eat and how much? What diet should we follow? What's too fat? What's too thin? Should we exercise? How much? What kind of exercise? And on and on it goes. We now have anorexia and bulimia, while at the same time, obesity and diabetes are at an all-time high. It's a sign of the times: We either try to escape into self-gratification or self-abuse when we can't gain control of our lives. In other words, if we can't control what's going on around us, we *can* control what goes (or doesn't go) into our mouths. Eating disorders have become an epidemic like drug abuse, and they're by-products of the enormous stress we all face these days.

Let's say that we charted to become heavy or thin, but the learning process is to get over it. We're given all of these lessons to overcome or deal with, not to let them destroy us, make us impotent, or delay our spiritual learning. Yes, we pick these good and bad (sometimes horrific) things, but they're just chosen for us to get through them, overcome them, and then become better for them. If they bring us to our spirituality, that's where the soul progresses up. If we're defeated, we haven't necessarily failed, but we *have* lost a great opportunity to advance our soul's spirituality.

On this level, we may also experience the fabled "seven-year itch." (The name is erroneous because it can come at any time.) We get bored because the newness has worn off of our marriage. Family or just life has crowded in, and if we're not careful, we start feeling that we can do better. Now if it's an impossible, abusive, addictive, or manipulative situation, dissatisfaction can strike at 7 years or 17—but just because we're bored, hit a bump in the road, or go through hard times, that's no reason to cash a basically good relationship in.

During adulthood we can also hit the menopausal or midlife-crisis period. Women go through their hormonal flux much like puberty, but now it's more intense. The biological clock has wound down, and sometimes the libido goes with it . . . only to be replaced by mood swings, weight gain, hot flashes, and other biological changes. Men go through this, too, but in different ways. Their midlife challenge is mental rather than physical, but they also become aware of their mortality and what they haven't accomplished. In other words, this is the time when everyone can go a little nuts—men run off with younger women, and women can find younger men. It's almost like trying to capture a dream that didn't come true before.

Reality is what it says: real. Don't let the world pull you away for a fantasy. Not only that, but no one builds happiness on someone else's pain. We have to go on, and not just because we're looking for some pot of gold at the end of some rainbow that doesn't even exist. As my grandmother used to say, "Do something in haste and repent in leisure." Through all this morass of life—with its tragedies, misfortunes, joys, and happiness—we do learn, but hopefully we do so with some dignity, too.

≈≈≈

On any level, but especially in adulthood, we can hit patches of quiet, happiness, trauma, and illness (be it ourselves or others around us), or financial desperation or affluence. We also have times of inertia, depression, and failure or accomplishment— along with "desert" or "survival" periods. Anyone who lives at all in the world will hit most all of these periods in large and small degrees. In adulthood, we're more aware of them because we're so ensconced in what's going on around us. When we're younger, emotions can pass as fast as a cloud passes the sun—it's not so with adult life and its needs to hang on and create stress.

— The quiet periods seem to be fewer and farther apart in our hectic society, but we must make way for them, even if it's for a few hours to just let ourselves exhale. The happy times can be spent with family and friends having conversations, eating meals, or just spending time together.

— Traumatic incidents can come to all of us, whether it's thanks to finances, societal pressures, or divorce or death. No one who lives for any length of time escapes these rough spots. Some individuals may even be sick for years, and people wonder why they'd choose that, but it's to perfect. It may seem as if some individuals' charts read worse than others, but please don't feel that they're bad or are being punished . . . they simply picked a difficult chart to perfect faster.

— We may also be faced with the care of our elderly parents; I personally had mine with me until I was 58. I didn't resent it, but it *was* an emotional and financial drain. I took on a lot of the care myself, but when I was working I had to have hospice come in and help me a few days a week. Then there were trips to the doctor and hospital, making sure that my mom and dad got their nutritional needs and prescriptions filled (and I don't even want to get into the Medicare situation and what they would or wouldn't cover).

— Then we have the desert periods, which seem to be filled with nothingness. We don't know where to go or what to do, and it's like we're in a wasteland with no relief in sight. I happen to feel that instead of looking at these as negative times, we should see them as respites from life's heavy schedule. We can write, paint, take walks, and relax and read to wait them out . . . because they *will* end. In desert periods it's as if all the clocks have stopped, as opposed to the survival times, in which we're running so fast that we never seem to get anything done. If we're smart, we shut the proverbial treadmill off and revamp what's important and where our priorities lie, even if it means cutting back on all the things we think we can't live without.

Remember that when we're going through depression, inertia, or even crushing sameness, we're actually learning all those miserable things we don't want to learn, such as patience; tolerance; survival; endurance; and, hopefully, spiritual knowledge. None of these times are without great merit because, again, they hone the soul for perfection.

I read for many people, and lots of times what we see from the outside doesn't always reflect what's happening on the inside. In other words, whether someone is wealthy or famous doesn't keep them from escaping the traumas, desert periods, or depressions. By the same token, when I'm lecturing to three or four thousand people, I sometimes ask to see a show of hands of those who feel more tired, stressed, depressed, or anxious than they ever have. I swear to you that 90 percent of the audience will raise their hands—and 10 or 20 years ago, this never was the case. It just shows what a jungle of survival our society is. Even though we've charted our lives, that doesn't mean that we can't learn by somewhat dropping out or down and reevaluating our lives and deciding not to keep up with the rest of the stampeding herd. We can still learn without being frantic.

I've personally gone through deaths, divorces, rejection, skepticism—you name it—and I've found that you can either stop at the first bump in the road or ride it through to the end. You'll face what you have to sooner or later (better sooner rather than later). So many times I've tried to skirt things or avoid them, but damn it if they don't inevitably revolve around again until I have no choice but to confront them. There's no easy way out of the chart we've written for ourselves, and delaying things only makes it harder. It's like a test we have to take: We can put it off and then agonize over the taking it, or we can just do it, and then it's done and over with. I've learned to do the tough or unpleasant tasks now—that way, I feel more relieved and don't have to obsess about them.

Remember that aside from dealing with everyday survival, problems, abusive behavior, children, parents, death, rejection, and financial worries, life still has its joys and euphoric periods, and sometimes when things get bad, we should bring up these times to soothe the pain of what's going on at the moment. When

I was going through a painful time after a surgery, I'd put myself in a daydream or meditative state and summon up quiet, lovely memories, and it really helped. This is in part how biofeedback works in healing—you place your mind somewhere else so that the afflicted part can heal.

Don't you find it amazing that you can cut yourself and don't know it, but the moment you see it or it's pointed out to you, it hurts? Sometimes I think ignorance truly is bliss. In fact, with certain people, the less they know, the better off they are. I don't mean that you should lie to anyone, but with those who are easily programmed, it's best to be judicious. Some doctors have even told me that they often withhold the more serious side of an illness to patients and more times than not, they get better.

Prayers truly only affect *us*. God doesn't need them, but they do elevate us to Him and makes His grace descend on us easier. Notice that people with a great sense of *knowing* (I like this word better than *faith*) handle life's adversities better because they have a working relationship with God. This type of relationship makes God closer to us because we've reached up to Him, our angels, and our guides, and it's easier for them to reach us through our belief—it helps thin the veil that separates us.

As for me, knowing that I have a chart is comforting, and I don't have a feeling of being controlled. Besides, who's controlling you but you and your own chart? It's like a fail-safe—you'll graduate, like it or not, and you may have delays, lateral movement, and even some interruptions, but the main courses that your soul needs to learn and expand will lift you up in perfection.

Chapter 9

The Seventh Level— Old Age

The final stages of life on Earth can actually be the most difficult (although I certainly don't mean to disregard all of the hardships we've experienced on the other levels). It's like Charles Dickens's *A Christmas Carol,* when the Ghost of Christmas Past came to show Ebenezer Scrooge his life in a montage of what he'd reaped or sown.

I touched on financial challenges in the last chapter, but on this level, they become more apparent and even frightening. Do we retire or do we keep on going to work? As I stated in the last chapter, retirement is great if we have something of interest to do or a long-awaited passion that we can indulge in. If it makes us money, all the better, but if *all* our needs are met, that is truly bliss.

If a husband dies and leaves the wife with very little cash (or illness has eaten up any kind of savings), this can be a scary scenario, just as if we retire early and don't have enough to live on. The idea of depending on our children is repugnant to most of us, as is the very real possibility of losing our independence.

It's hard to put away money at this time. Whether we're alone or have a family, the cost of living can be prohibitive. Yet some of us go too far and keep giving to our kids, not realizing that we're ensuring that we have no cushion—and then, in the blink of an eye, we're older and have nothing for ourselves. I'm not an advocate of so-called tough love, but if we keep carrying our children, they'll take it for granted, and then their own legs won't work anymore. Sometimes responsibility has to be taught, and this age-old belief that we'll get paid back on loans made to children is almost never adhered to. We're not a bank where there's nothing but withdrawals and no deposits.

As we near the end of our lives, we start thinking about our legacy—where will our money go and who deserves it? Will there be bickering over what we have (or what the family thinks we have)? If we're smart, it isn't morbid to make a will early on in adulthood. We can always add to or subtract from it later on, add a codicil, or even change it completely. Trust funds are also good, especially for grandchildren, as the money can mature and then be withdrawn for college or whatever is needed.

In fact, the one great joy we older people have is grandchildren, who are blessings from God. Perhaps we enjoy them so much because we're not in the mode of survival that we were in when we were raising our own kids. Now we have the time to talk and be with our grandchildren without the worry of work or providing food, clothing, and shelter. Recently, a study in a scientific journal stated that we often see ourselves more in our grandchildren than we do in our own children. True or not, there are definite signs of this for me: My granddaughter loves to write and perform, and my grandsons have a wicked sense of humor. I also showed signs of being more like Grandma Ada than I did my parents in temperament, psychic ability, humanitarian thrust, and interest in literature.

If we don't have any offspring, many times we're aunts or uncles, godparents, or neighbors, and that's how we interact with younger ones and give them our love. We also have our loving pets. People who don't have them don't understand how we can feel that they're part of the family; but they truly are loving, loyal angels on Earth who give us nothing but unconditional love. They don't have to come back and reincarnate because they don't have a chart . . . except to give humankind enjoyment. We also don't become animals—just as we don't become angels—for there is no transmigration of souls.

❧◦◦◦☙

Once we reach this final level on Earth, not only are we getting older, but we may also have health problems (which can be debilitating to say the least, especially if care and help are needed). Let's face it, years ago people died in their 40s. Now we're living longer—insurance companies offering life-insurance policies to the elderly have made that apparent—and we're also quickly getting to the point where the elderly are starting to comprise the bulk of the population because of the baby-boomer generation. This is a double-edged sword: It's great that our medicine has advanced to keep us alive longer; but it's also created a burden on HMOs, Social Security, and retirement funds.

Of course most people on Social Security get anywhere from $10,000 to $15,000 per year, which isn't exactly a living wage in this country. Consequently, many senior citizens find themselves in the unaccustomed role of having to rely on others for just about everything. Depression is a very real situation in those who lose their independence; and, unfortunately, here in the United States we look at these folks as being a disposable burden. Other cultures care for their elderly and revere them much more than we do.

The aspect that's most frustrating for the elderly (at least in my case) is the loss of mobility and energy. As we get older, our energy begins to wane; our endurance is not as strong, even if we push ourselves (which I constantly find myself doing); and our range of motion is greatly decreased. Small aches and pains that we'd slough off when we were younger now force us to sit or lie down. A walk or hike that was a breeze earlier in life now becomes a test of endurance with frequent stops and rests. For most of us, sports such as baseball, football, tennis, and basketball are now only enjoyed as spectators. Golf we can sometimes do, but only with a cart that can follow those 50-yard drives that are poked out there with creaky joints and sore muscles.

I'm exaggerating here (I think), but to those of us who've been active all our lives, this is an especially bitter pill to swallow. I know that there are some seniors out there who are in great shape and still party with the best of them, but they're in the minority. Usually most of us don't realize our age (or we try not to), so we become frustrated with some of our limitations. It can be as simple as getting on or off the floor or even being in a restaurant booth and finding that we just don't bound up like we used to. I used to jump out of bed, and now it's more of a scoot.

Years ago my abusive first husband threw me against a wall, injuring my leg right below the hip joint. It hurt for a while, so I got it x-rayed, and I was told that it looked like a hairline fracture and that I should stay off it as much as possible (yeah, right!). I asked Francine if it would give me problems, and she replied, "Not until you get older." Then when I was 67, my leg started to hurt below the hip, especially if I walked a long distance. I was really aggravated and barked at Francine, "You told me this wouldn't bother me until I got older!"

Her smart retort was, "And you are how old now?" *Damn!* I said to myself. I never really thought of myself as "older." My injury isn't desperate, but it does make me look as if I'm waddling sometimes. Healing meditation has eased it some, but soon there will be a type of glue invented that doctors can inject to help. The only reason I mention this is because none of us are impervious to problems as we get older. Sometimes I feel that the body was only supposed to last a certain amount of years. . . .

Bodily ills can be painful, but they're easier to live with than mental deterioration is. When mental problems occur, extra care is needed—we have the option of assisted living or even a nursing home if we become incapacitated. (I feel that a nursing home should be the last resort or to be used only in the very last stages of life—keep in mind that hospice is also an option.) When the quality of life is no longer there, we can ask for a DNR (do not resuscitate), which just means that God's will be done. Personally, I think that we keep life going too long when there's no joy left. No, I don't believe in assisted death, but don't keep me alive with mechanical means when I can't think or function on my own.

Much more than we used to see, people are allowed to go home to die these days, which is better for the person passing on, as loved ones are around and they don't have to endure the cold, impersonal environment of a hospital room. (As an aside, when we die we're surrounded by our passed-over loved ones, angels, guides, Mother and Father God, and Jesus—just as we are in life. We are *never* alone.) If our spirituality is high and we know that we're going to the Other Side, we can will ourselves to go, especially if we haven't been too caught up in the "things" of life.

Death certainly shouldn't be a burden, either financially or otherwise. If an elderly person has nothing left, then the family has to figure out how to bury him or her with dignity. I really don't think funerals should be so expensive, but many companies use guilt to sell. If we don't have the best casket with all the pomp and ceremony, we feel that we're doing a disservice to our dead loved ones. Well, I've never talked to anyone on the Other Side who cared what was done with them after they went Home. They're also never mad at us concerning what we do with their money or any personal effects. They don't hold grudges, are never disappointed with us, and aren't upset that we didn't get a chance to say good-bye. Otherwise, it wouldn't be heaven—everyone would be upset and hanging on to resentment instead of being in a perfect and loving environment that holds nothing but happiness and joy.

If someone asks me if his or her loved ones made it Home and I say yes, invariably the next question is, "Are they happy?" Well, of course they are—that's what heaven means! Many times well-meaning family members can actually be the hardest to deal with during the death of a loved one. They beg the person to stay, so he or she hangs on out of love. Yet the kindest thing you can do for your dying loved ones is talk them over to the Other Side, telling them that everything will be all right and that you and your family will be fine. Then there's no guilt or sorrow for the person who's leaving.

It's very much like going on a joyous trip and having it spoiled by the whole family hanging on you and crying and telling you how much they'll miss you—that's what you'd take with you on the journey. Of course this is no longer true once they get into the tunnel to go over there, but it sure makes the first step of soul separating from the body harder.

If a soul does get caught in between here and Home, then we can do our best to release them to the light. However, this occurrence is very rare because over 99 percent of all people make it over without any problem. The reason we hear about ghosts is because it gives humans hope that we do survive. If people see or are aware of a ghost, then they surmise that *they* can live on, too. That's why ghosts are so fascinating. Yet eventually someone comes to get them, and even they go back to the Other Side. So when your time comes to pass, always remember to go toward the light, and you'll enter a tunnel filled with love and joy and proceed quickly to all those who await you in unending bliss.

There really isn't any reason that you can't die with dignity, no matter what illness you have. It's a matter of knowing where you're going and then willing yourself to just let go. Guides, family members, close friends, angels, and God are all there—as are your pets and the loved ones you haven't incarnated with—just waiting to see you again.

❧❧

Now the levels we endure on this planet are complete. In other words, we've come full circle from birth to rebirth by going back Home. All the scenarios I've illustrated in this part are an overview of what so many of us go through during the different phases of our charted learning process to gain spirituality, grace, and advancement and learning for our soul. All lives are different, but there *is* a commonality in the stages we all go through. For example, we can't help mourning the loss of a loved one, and grief is real and tangible—it lies like a dragon deep in our solar plexus, waiting to rise up at any moment to devour us.

Yet even in our later years, when we see so many of our friends and loved ones die, it makes things easier when we realize that we're really only here for a blink of God's eye . . . and then we go Home and are in such a state of bliss. We're so proud of ourselves that we were brave enough to come down to this hell to survive and expand our knowledge, awareness, and spirituality. We go back to the *real* reality of living and learning, in that perfect and beautiful place with no negativity that we call the Other Side.

It makes me crazy when people get down on themselves and say that all they've done is live, work, and take care of their loved ones. To survive each level of life is a big job, and we do the best we can. And who would trade in hearing a baby's laugh, holding a puppy or a loved one's hand, or seeing the face of a beloved friend?

In my case, the rush of going onstage and seeing your beautiful faces, the letters I get, and even the pleasure of giving a reading to someone and presenting them with answers or peace is the joy that fills my soul. Even as I write these words, I'm delighted, as I hope that someone reading them will seek the knowledge I have (like Jesus taught us to do), which will bring not just hope but conviction, too.

Every one of us has to go through tough times, but we must find our passion and joy and not sweat the small stuff or worry about things that won't happen. We have to remember that when we go Home to the Other Side, this Earthly life will have been like a dream—some of it bad, some good—but we'll have graduated, and that truly and simply is what it's all about. So let's keep on with our journey and know that we're all in it together, just as we all meet up together in God's beautiful domain.

PART III

THE SEVEN LEVELS
OF THE OTHER SIDE

Introduction to Part III

Now it's time to talk about one of my favorite subjects: the Other Side. This is the dimension of true reality, where we live for eternity with no negativity, and we bask in the love of God forever. The Other Side is not only made for God's creations, but it's truly a paradise in which we have bodies for our souls, magnificent buildings and structures, gorgeous and eternally flowering gardens, constant love and light, and the splendor of nature in all its glory.

In fact, nothing of the natural beauty of Earth is left out: We still have the Grand Canyon, the oceans, Yellowstone and Yosemite National Parks, Niagara and Victoria Falls, the Himalayas, the Alps, the hills of Umbria, and on and on it goes. Beauteous works of humankind that no longer exist, such as the Hanging Gardens of Babylon or the Colossus of Rhodes, are also still present on the Other Side. *Anything* that is of beauty or magnificence is there for us to enjoy . . . whether or not it's actually on the planet anymore.

The Other Side consists of seven levels, and for the purpose of clarification, I must stress that the word *level* in this instance doesn't mean that one is better than another. Rather, I'm using the term to signify a separate area or division, much like I've divided this book into chapters. In other words, a soul on the third level can be just as advanced as one on the sixth and so forth. Most of the levels can be defined as our "vocation" on the Other Side—that is, what we love to do and feel best suited for.

We get so used to looking at numbers to delineate quality or advancement here on this plane of existence called Earth. Even when I was teaching, we'd divide the children by their reading skills using birds' names. The "Robins" were the best readers, while those who found it most difficult were the "Redbirds," with the "Blue Jays" somewhere in between. (I'm sure that they figured it out, but at least the other teachers and I tried very hard to keep the Redbirds from feeling inferior.) Please don't take this formula and apply it to the Other Side because it just isn't true. An advanced soul can be on any level.

Now, since our Home is our reality, the Earth plane basically mirrors it as far as topography is concerned—but this planet is just not as perfect or beautiful as the Other Side, nor does it have many of its components. For example, while there are seven continents on Earth, the Other Side has nine, counting the lost lands of Atlantis and Lemuria. Each of these continents is then divided into four areas or "quadrants." Although each quadrant is basically a delineation for housing a particular level, you'll find entities from all levels in all quadrants, but the bulk of entities in a particular quadrant will be whatever that area's level delineation is.

In other words, the quadrant that's designated for fourth-level entities will have the majority of its population consisting of similar folks, with a smattering of those from other levels. This is essentially done for interaction of the populace with similar interests. However, it's also expedient for the housing of animals in topography that's best for them, as well as having buildings for similar purposes (such as research) close to each other. Quadrants help organize the activities and various populations on the Other Side, which makes for greater efficiency.

As individual entities, we also reside in homes or domiciles in a particular quadrant on a particular continent, but we can go from one quadrant to another by just thinking ourselves there. We may live in the area of Asia, for instance, and want to visit a research center in the vicinity of California—well, in the blink of an eye, we'd be there! As mentioned earlier, we can also bilocate if we so choose. So if we're doing research and want to hear a concert or a lecture at the same time, we can do so. I know that it's hard for us to understand this concept, but most us who multitask regularly can understand it to some extent. For example, I can have the TV on and still write and answer my phone. Over on the Other Side, we use all of our brains, instead of just a tenth of it, as we do here. So what we're capable of doing is almost limitless. . . .

Let's now look at each level in further detail.

CHAPTER 10

THE FIRST LEVEL—
THE TRANSITIONAL STATE

The first level we're going to look at isn't really a level as such. It's actually just the transitional state from life on Earth to that on the Other Side, the so-called way station for outgoing and incoming souls. You see, some are leaving Home to complete their charts—they're off with what they've contracted to do to learn for God, perfect their souls, and gain more knowledge. They've got their themes (their purposes), which carry all the joys, pains, and nuances that make up the life they've contracted for in a new incarnation. Meanwhile, the incoming souls carry with them all the knowledge that they've acquired from their just-lived life on Earth and are ecstatic to be back Home . . . hopefully much wiser and with their souls expanded from what they've just gone through.

This is a challenging level, especially for the outgoing entities who are going into an Earth life. The soul's entrance and departure from life on Earth is seemingly hard both ways, but death isn't nearly as difficult as birth is. I know you'll tell me that you've sat beside a loved one who passed and seemingly saw his or her pain.

Well, in 50 years of talking to probably as many departed souls as living, no one has ever told me that they had a terrible or even a painful death.

I believe that what you may have seen is the separation of your loved one's soul from his or her body, but the soul is more or less oblivious to it. I even asked my guide Francine if God in His mercy makes the people forget or puts them in an amnesic state. She said no, that regardless of what we may see, the person's essence isn't disturbed by what the body is going through. She likened it to a chicken with its head cut off: Even after the head is severed, the body kicks or runs around, but the chicken itself is gone.

≈◦≈

When we die, we do go through the tunnel (I've personally had this happen twice in near-death situations), and many children who have had such experiences also mention a bridge with a rainbow over it. It always reminds me of the famous picture of an angel helping children across a bridge that used to hang in many Catholic schoolrooms. In that depiction, the bridge looked broken, which was supposed to indicate the guardian angel's protection—but I think it shows what happens when a little one makes the transition Home.

Doctors and other health workers (including myself) find that death is much easier for the very young and often the very old. I can understand this because the young have so recently come from the Other Side, while the elderly are usually quite ready to go—to the point that they often even see their relatives coming to get them. Yet for those of us who fall in the middle, we're more entrenched in life, so it tends to be much harder for us to let go and leave to go back Home.

Whenever we do travel through the tunnel, we don't go alone. Our guide, angels, loved ones who have passed before us, and the many we know and love greet us and help us make the transition.

(Most people fail to think about the myriad souls on the Other Side who never incarnate with us, yet many are often closer to us than anyone on the Earth plane is.) There are usually hundreds of people and pets awaiting anyone who passes over to celebrate their homecoming . . . and many times, there's a giant party to boot!

It's true that some entities don't make it through the tunnel, but it's such a rarity that the number is practically insignificant. Still, it's enough for those who have had a loved one die by their own hands or in other traumatic ways to be concerned as to whether or not he or she made it Home. Well, many suicides *do* make it because they're sick from either being bipolar or emotionally deranged, so they're not responsible for their actions.

I understand when people ask me if a passed-over loved one made it, but I don't get why when I say yes, they then ask me if the deceased is happy. No matter how someone may have died, the Other Side is a paradise where there's *no negativity of any kind.* Therefore, anyone who dies and makes it over there is happy beyond all our dreams and expectations; after all, they're back in the real life that God made for us all. We'll all go back Home at one time or another, and when we do, we'll become ecstatic beyond our wildest dreams.

Imagine a reality in which we no longer experience the negative human emotions of jealousy, hate, greed, laziness, prejudice, envy, anger, and the like. We don't have to eat or sleep . . . we can assume any looks or body we wish . . . we can choose our friends and loved ones without any repercussions . . . we can work at anything we want, with total satisfaction and the necessary talent to do so . . . we can dance, sing, laugh, and hold intimate and meaningful conversations . . . we can study and research to our heart's content . . . and on and on it goes. Think of anything that brings you joy and you can do it!

The Other Side is the true utopia of creation, and as such, most entities (except for spirit guides) tend to be less empathetic and concerned with the plight of those of us still on Earth. It's not that they don't love and care for us, but they know that this plane is just transitory. Also, with all the knowledge available to them, they know what we must go through, but they also know that we'll make it and be back with them in a very short period. There's no such thing as time in this paradise, so 50 years to us is like a few weeks to them—and what's a few weeks in the scheme of eternity?

You can see why those on the Other Side wouldn't be too concerned with the everyday events of our Earth lives, especially when they know that we'll be with them soon. Sure, they'll look in on us from time to time, but they also know that what has happened to them will soon happen to us and that we'll be as blissfully euphoric when we return Home as they are. I liken it to parents tending scraped knees on their children. They know it's not serious and that the kids will get over it in a short period of time and will go on their merry way again.

Amazingly, all the things you've worried about slip away as you go through the tunnel, and you just know that everything everywhere will be all right. There's such a sense of utter knowing, well-being, and blessed relief from all of life's problems. It's hard to imagine unless you've done it, but through my extensive research, I've found that everyone, without one exception, describes these same feelings (in regression, the astral state, or even in the vivid dream state) whenever they're visiting the Other Side.

As you progress through the tunnel, which is very bright, you see the end of it as an even brighter light. As you get closer, you can only make out silhouetted forms at first, but as you get closer you begin to discern the faces of your passed-over loved ones. You're also aware that as you go through the tunnel, you're getting younger and younger until you reach the age of 30. If you're younger than 30 when you pass, you'll get a bit older and more mature until you again reach 30, which is how old we all are on the Other Side.

People frequently ask me how they're going to recognize someone whom they only knew either at an older or younger age, such as a grandparent or childhood friend. First of all, you must remember that the Other Side is your Home and you know everyone over there—even if everyone is 30 years of age, you'll instantly recognize the soul as they look at that age. You'll also experience your mind opening up totally, and with that change in brainpower comes the recognition of souls no matter what they look like. And last but not least, if you're a little hesitant in going toward the light, passed-over loved ones will assume the visage of how you last remembered them in your Earth life to make it easier for you to gravitate toward them. This doesn't have to be done often because those on the Other Side are almost always recognized by the incoming soul before this has to take place.

We all exist for eternity at Home, we know all the souls that we come in contact with there, and our memory is so expanded that we remember them easily. Even children are easily recognizable there because before we all incarnated, we charted our lives and how they interacted. We were all 30 when we did this, and of course we knew each other. It's only on Earth that we age, become ill, and die—never when we're on the Other Side. We have to stop thinking of this planet as the ultimate place of knowing . . . it isn't. We've had many lives and souls still recognize each other. It's that instant recognition of "I've always known you," whether it's from another life or our ultimate Home.

My granddaughter told me an interesting story once. She said that she felt as if she had a "type of dream" in which she went to the Other Side and was watching through a window where she saw a lot of babies. She asked someone if she could go in there and was told no, because the babies were ready to go into life.

I went back to Francine and said, "I thought that we're all 30 on the Other Side." She replied that we are until we're ready to incarnate. At that point, we're put in the "baby state" so that our souls are acclimated and orientated to coming into life. However, they're still in a holding state at this level. (As an aside, so many parents are truly and rightly in such grief from having a stillborn infant or miscarriage, but all my research has discovered that in those situations, the entity never even comes in. I checked with Francine, and she stated that this was true because no soul learns anything from an unfulfilled life.)

So even though it's transitory, this level is very important to both outgoing and incoming souls. It's the last stop before a person goes into an incarnation to learn for God, as well as the first stop for a soul coming Home. I can't stress enough that this area gives both the outgoing and incoming souls a tremendous shock, in the sense that the difference in how someone feels between the Other Side and the Earth plane is sometimes beyond comprehension. Our souls aren't acclimated to the tremendous difference between a realm of no negativity and one in which it runs rampant. Thank God that we only have to leave and experience that hell for a short period to learn and that we have such a wonderful and beautiful Home to come back to!

～⌘～

CHAPTER 11

THE SECOND LEVEL— ORIENTATION

The second level on the Other Side is actually the orientation process, which can take many forms. As I mentioned in the last chapter, when we emerge from the tunnel we generally have an immediate reunion with our loved ones and pets. This meeting can be brief or extended, but eventually we start an orientation process that's different for each soul—just as each soul is unique unto itself. This is not only a learning process of becoming reoriented back Home, but it's also a healing process that helps alleviate some of the soul trauma that occurs from incarnation and when a soul switches between dimensions that are so different in nature.

Your spirit guide may immediately take you to the Hall of Wisdom, a beautiful, white Romanesque building with gleaming pillars and marble steps leading up to huge golden doors that swing open when you approach. You're then escorted into a room that you're familiar with after many lives. There's a domed ceiling that emits prisms of brilliant light, and you sit quietly on a marble bench and watch a video screen that appears from the floor. You'll view your just-lived existence in 3-D, almost as if you're there, yet you're just an observer. By this time, it's just you and the presence of God who are observing your whole life.

Now if you lived to be 80 years old, that doesn't mean that you'll sit there for 80 years—remember that time doesn't really exist on the Other Side. Also, your brainpower is now 100 percent, so you can observe and absorb information more quickly and accurately. You're literally scanning your life (which is why they call this screen mechanism "the scanning machine"), but with more detail and accuracy than you could ever hope to obtain on the Earth plane.

You observe every part of your life, including your actions and influences, along with what you *didn't* do, and you make mental notes. Our minds are so much more expanded on the Other Side that this is enough. (In this life, you'd probably fill several notebooks with copious notes and go over and over different areas of life to remember what you would have or should have done, or to mentally "save" the good parts.)

What you feel you should have done and the joy of what you did do survive—of course you have feelings, but you don't experience pain, rejection, or sorrow again. I guess I'd say that you look at things from a more clinical perspective; in other words, there's no stomping around, putting your head in your hands, or cursing yourself for your stupidity. There's no one to criticize you, no voice from God booms that you ought to be ashamed. Instead, you're more interested in the fact that you stayed close to your previously written chart. You realize where your strengths and weaknesses were, but through it all you have a sense of joy that you were brave enough to even go down to Earth for God. It's truly a time of reflection on your just-lived existence, and lost or fuzzy memories become clear again without any suffering.

After that facet of Orientation is over, your guide escorts you to the Hall of Justice—another Romanesque building that also looks as if it has prisms of light that emanate from the pinkish-looking marble—where the Council resides. The Council is a group of very advanced souls (also called "the Brotherhood" or "Avatars" or "Elders") who have been picked by God as advisors and are very evolved and spiritual. They're also the only ones on the Other Side who look older, which delineates their wisdom. They dress in white robes with golden sashes and sit at such a table that allows you to walk in the middle of them, with these dear entities gathered all around you.

All people on all levels are privy to going to the Council if they so desire, and whether it's constructing a chart for a proposed life or reviewing one just lived, their wisdom is invaluable. At Orientation, you're asked to speak about your life and what you decided to accomplish before you came in, and the Council reviews your chart with you—which, of course, they helped advise you on before you even went in to life. You're asked to explain how you think you did, yet in no way is this an adversarial proceeding; it's more like a loving critique and, if anything, is a kind and uplifting experience.

You're asked if you would have done a situation differently (and if so, how and why), and the Council takes your side whenever you may be too hard on yourself. They will also defend you if you say that you could have done better, and they'll gently lead you to a deeper understanding of why you may have missed some guideposts on your particular road. It truly is what it claims to be: counseling that informs and helps you see your experiences more clearly.

You're then given time to decide whether you want to go into life again. When I asked Francine how much time, she just said that it was tough to come up with a figure (in fact, she's often told me that one of the hardest things for her to do is to put a sequence of events in a time frame since it doesn't exist on the Other Side). However, she *could* give me the sequence of events after one leaves the Council. The average person who dies on the Earth plane takes approximately three days in our time to fully gather their complete essence after death, but this is like a minute or two on the Other

Side. This scenario of events or actions is typical of what most of us go through during orientation, but by no means is it written in stone. Some will go through a shorter process than others—it all depends on the individual's needs.

After you leave the session with the Council, you go out near the Hall of Justice, where there's a huge meadow and rose garden. You're then reunited in a very personal way with your closest intimates, and you may decide to be one-on-one with your soul mate for a while or talk with a small group of loved ones. You can also "merge" with other entities, and when you do, you'll get a real orgasmic feeling—but besides that, you'll share your just-lived experiences without their having to actually live them. (This is much easier than explaining what you've just been through to them.) You can also go back to the scanning machine with them and allow them to view parts or the whole of your life if it helps them learn.

To digress for a bit here, I can really relate to this process. You see, when something fantastic happens in our church, we may say to "flag" it, which means that these are special moments that we'd like to review again, let others see how we dealt with it, or note how the outcome affected other events. We even like sharing the funny and hysterical instances. It's like when something great happened to my boys or we were all together having a special time—I'd say, "Close your eyes and save this moment, so when life gets tough you can bring it out like a photo album in your mind and remember how you felt."

Back on the Other Side, you may next decide to go to what are called the Towers behind the Hall of Records, which is a massive Greek/Roman structure that contains all of the scrolls and records of lives. (It's also called the "Akashic Records," which are the recorded knowledge of all humankind from infinity, as well as every action related to humans, Earth, or the universe.) The Towers are beautiful Gothic-like structures where you can go and be quiet and meditate or contemplate. It's very monastic-looking inside, but it also has candles interspersed throughout, with beautiful light refractions from the windows and gorgeous fountains here and there, along with many little alcoves for privacy.

∽⤳ ⤲∼

In some cases, entities may come back from Earth and be what's called "cocooned." This happens when souls have been very traumatized in their just-lived lives. This doesn't necessarily mean that they've had a harsh or even painful crossing—it could be the result of a very quick passing or a life in which they had many scars put on their soul. Such entities are placed in a sleeplike state in an enclosed chamber and given a form of therapy to heal any trauma they may have endured. The orientation process is slower for these cocooned entities, but since we know that there's no time on the Other Side, it still happens very quickly. Eventually, they're awakened and can see their loved ones and go into the Hall of Wisdom to review their lives, but with now-healed minds and souls.

This process of cocooning is very loving. I liken it to when I've been on a particularly exhausting lecture and book-signing tour. It's nice to go home to my own bed and just go "flat" for a short time, to rest, sleep, and rejuvenate until I feel like resuming my normal activities. That's the kind of therapy worn-out and traumatized souls receive on the Other Side.

Entities that have been tortured or traumatized to the point where their minds have been affected are normally cocooned, but so are some people who are very attached to someone who's still in life—such as my own father. It was ten months in my time before I could even contact him, which Francine said was done because it was so hard for him to leave me. Even though there's no fear, longing, or guilt on the Other Side, such entities are cocooned so that their reorientation is easier and their comfort is assured. To be cocooned is not a stigma of any kind, and Francine has said that no one has ever been in such a state for years and years in our time (which would be like a few days to them). We should just think of this as a rest station, in which the individuals concerned are warm, comforted, and cared for.

While cocooning isn't a rare occurrence, most entities tend to "hit the ground running"—that is, they go through the tunnel, say hello to their animals and loved ones, go into the Hall of Wisdom, and then come out and resume the activities that they left behind. So this second level is a fairly quick one because it's a genuinely happy process of getting used to an environment without the negativity of the life we just came from. This is a place to collect and reorient ourselves before we move on to the next levels.

Chapter 12

The Third Level— Animal Husbandry and Horticulture

When we're Home, we work at what we have a passion for, and we're ecstatically happy in all of our pursuits. I'm positive that most entities carry their love of a certain type of work with them when they come down into the Earth plane, and if we're lucky, we get to do what we so enjoy on the Other Side down here.

No matter what level we're on, we can visit, work, and have loved ones on different levels. In other words, there's no "class distinction" between the levels. When I go to the Other Side, I tend to be on the sixth level (that of teachers and lecturers), but I often visit this third one as well, for it's where all the work in foliage, flowers, and gardening is being done. It's also where the animals are. And while some entities on this level multitask—like taking care of animals while simultaneously doing research in some other field—most are content to do their work and research in the same area.

You simply can't imagine the beauty that those in horticulture create: There are new species of orchids, and every plant you could ever conceive of is created and cared for. The flowers can grow seven or eight feet tall, bugs don't exist, and there aren't any diseases such as fungus. Even though I've been told that there are no insects as such, the plants must have a way of pollinating (whoops—I fell into the trap of thinking that the Other Side is like Earth again!). Although gardeners aren't needed here to maintain the countless beautiful flora that abounds, many choose to do so simply because they love it.

This level also has many researchers in the animal and horticulture fields. Behavior is studied, although it's somewhat limited because instinctual actions such as hunting aren't done on the Other Side and animal communication isn't a mystery— any person can understand any creature and vice versa. There are many activities done with the animals, though, such as horseback and show riding, dog shows and grooming, and so forth. Entities on this level can train animals, ride them, play with them, and even interact with them, although the interaction never reaches the level of that with a fellow human being . . . after all, the Other Side isn't Narnia.

❧❧

People on this level take care of all creatures, including those that were wild and didn't have an owner in life, as well as the ones that choose to stay and wait for their loved ones. Now many people over the years have expressed their concern to me about their beloved pets that passed on. They worry if the animals have survived death and whether their owners will be able to find or recognize them on the Other Side. Well, they do, and you will. In fact, some animals will stay with relatives or loved ones on the Other Side who were familiar with them on Earth.

I will say once and for all here that animals don't reincarnate, nor would they need to. They have a one-shot life and don't have anything to learn because they're already God's perfect intellectual and instinctual creatures. They don't project avarice, greed, or jealousy; and they've been placed on Earth to aid humankind. Wild animals are a source of food for us, and they help our environment by keeping nature in balance (while human beings keep putting it *out of* balance). The domesticated ones such as cows, pigs, and sheep also serve as food and can even help clothe us. When it comes to pets, however, they simply give us devoted companionship and hours upon hours of loving pleasure and entertainment.

Animals, for the most part, have been treated unkindly by humans, and I really believe that renegade creatures have become that way because our encroachment and cruelty has turned them into entities that must fight for survival. However, the caregivers of these blessed creatures tend to them lovingly on the Other Side. It's not even unusual to see a monkey on the back of a Bengal tiger, holding on to its ears as the giant cat gallops through wilderness areas or gardens. In fact, all of God's magnificent creations play and interact with each other constantly—and with no need to eat or sleep. Instinctual survival is not an issue.

Many entities on the Other Side make special trips to view and interact with the animals. To see vast herds and groups of these magnificent creatures in the wonderful beauty of nature is truly a treat. Extinct species such as dinosaurs are also there and are some of the favorites for viewing. The millions upon millions of different animal species—as well as the countless fish and birds that are in the oceans and sky—are there for us to enjoy, study, and gaze upon.

Most of the creatures on the Other Side reside in the same area, and you may wonder how so many of them can live in what you may perceive as a limited space. Again, the Other Side isn't like Earth. Just as time doesn't exist there, neither do the limitations of geography.

It's difficult to explain, but spatial physics is different on the Other Side—there's *never* any crowding. Many of you have heard the old adage of 10,000 angels sitting on the head of a pin; well, it's much the same on our Home. Millions of God's creations cohabitate in what seems like a limited area with no overcrowding; with vast areas of wilderness, mountains, lakes, rivers, streams, oceans, and beaches that exhibit the rich beauty of nature; along with gorgeous gardens and magnificent structures in which we all reside. This is truly a paradise, and it's so spectacularly breathtaking that words cannot describe it.

CHAPTER 13

THE FOURTH LEVEL—
ARTISTIC AND
AESTHETIC PURSUITS

On the fourth level we encounter writers, painters, sculptors, composers, musicians, singers, poets, and entertainers; along with artisans, craftspeople, and architects who deal with wood, brick, clay, marble, or any other medium that helps people create something from their own designs or imagery.

This level also incorporates anyone in the building industry, fashion and interior designers, cabinetry and furniture makers, those who like to work with machinery, and even those who enjoy cooking and making up exotic cuisines. It's interesting to note that even though the Other Side has no need for many occupations such as chefs, accountants, mechanics, politicians, soldiers, and the like, many still work in these fields for the sheer love of it. These entities see the fruits of their labors realized in new designs or theories that come out on Earth. For example, a chef will experiment with different types of cuisine, and since we don't need to eat when we're Home, he or she may put a new recipe in the mind of someone who works in the culinary arts on Earth.

Now, someone like Beethoven comes in to life with the knowledge that he's acquired on the Other Side. Some individuals do bring things in with them from past lives, but I think we have to be aware of the fact that for eons of time we've been on the Other Side, so our acquired knowledge comes down with us when we incarnate. Think about Leonardo, Raphael, Michelangelo, and the other great artists and sculptors who are carrying on that legacy today; and look at all of the new architectural designs that have never been seen before. Where do you think these ideas are coming from? You guessed it—they're either being carried over or infused from the Other Side. The ancient architecture of the Greeks, Romans, and Egyptians are just copies of designs that have existed forever on our Home and were carried over to the Earth plane.

So we not only choose our lives when we incarnate, but we can bring marvelous knowledge with us, too. Unfortunately, we can also carry over a lot of negative things that have happened to us in past lives, which result in illness and phobias. I'm not saying that if you were a great writer in a past life you wouldn't carry that over as well—but don't negate the fact that you probably *are* a great writer or painter or whatever on the Other Side.

❦

Again and again in my readings, I'm seeing that there are increasing numbers of people coming in to life with very definitive artistic abilities. In fact, the whole culture that I see either wants to help make the world better through research or by bringing in beauty. Also, many entities are coming back from Atlantis and Lemuria, where knowledge reigned supreme. As Plato described them, these were places of beauty and advancement, but humankind's propensity for violence and the polar tilt destroyed them. Nevertheless, entities that lived there were able to bring over much of the areas' beauty and technology.

Speaking of Atlantis, Francine says that it was at one time so advanced, as far as supernatural knowledge and technological acumen go, that it was beyond anything we even know today. I think that at its peak, Atlantis was probably the one instance in which Earth mirrored the Other Side (or at least more than at any other time).

People think that those of us who believe in Atlantis are crazy, but this term was once applied to Christopher Columbus and Marco Polo as well. In the not-too-distant future, we'll find traces of Atlantis near the Greek island of Santorini. This discovery will give us an idea of what the Other Side looks like, as well as how similar Greek and Roman architecture is to the structures on our Home. (For more information on Atlantis and Lemuria, please see my book *Secrets & Mysteries of the World*.)

৩৩ ৩৩

CHAPTER 14

THE FIFTH LEVEL— SCIENTISTS, MISSION-LIFE ENTITIES, AND MYSTICAL TRAVELERS

The fifth level is the domain of what are known as "mission-life entities" and "mystical travelers," along with researchers, scientists, and certain types of counselors. This level has a lot of diversity and movement (as does the sixth)—many entities here multitask with other levels and even interchange levels depending on what they're doing. Conversely, while all levels have interaction, and some inhabitants change their areas depending on what they're doing, the third and fourth levels contain those who don't choose as much diversity as those on the fifth and sixth levels do.

There aren't as many mystical travelers as there are mission-life entities—and compared to the Other Side's population, there really aren't that many mission-life entities at all. Both types of souls are now trying to fulfill a chart dictating that Mother God be brought into the foreground in religion after being suppressed for so many centuries. The way you can tell these entities is by their search for spirituality and by the fact that they step away from the crowd. They come to bring humankind back to the reality of what God's all about and what we're here for. Like Joan of Arc, they're on a mission or have a focus to bring about what's right, no matter what the cost to them might be.

This doesn't mean that everyone who's been martyred are mission-life entities, but the chances are great that anyone who dies or even lives for a greater good is one. A mystical traveler, however, always creates a better understanding in the spiritual arena. Such an entity will go to any planet or galaxy where they're needed to bring about the understanding of God, love, and the journey of life and the hereafter.

Jesus Christ was a true mystical traveler, and it doesn't diminish him by saying that there are others here on Earth today, just as they've been since the beginning of humanity. Similarly, each religion has its own spokesperson: Through their lives and writings, Buddha, Mohammed, and countless others have tried to bring about a greater good.

Mission-life entities start out (not necessarily spiritually at first, but they always move into that area) wanting to help people, and they come in with knowledge about God, goodness, the Other Side, or just saving humanity in general. It's like when Martin Luther King, Jr., said, "I have a dream." It was one that he wanted to become a reality, in which *all* humankind—black, white, yellow, red, and brown—would get along and love each other, for we're all created by our almighty God. (Not to be negative, but notice how many of these entities suffer a lot or even give up their lives. Well, sometimes they see and feel so much that their lives are full of great anguish.)

Mission-life entities and mystical travelers may feel somewhat reluctant after they get down to Earth because their lives are often up for grabs. This doesn't mean that they don't have a chart . . . it's just all over the place. They're out there helping, traveling, speaking, and writing, using any type of media to get their message out. And make no mistake about it—they charted this life for themselves.

Also, once this is imprinted on a soul, it can't be taken off. Only once have I heard of it taken back, and it was done to a person I happened to know. Nevertheless, this was the only time I ever heard of that happening because being a mystical traveler or mission-life entity takes a great commitment on that individual's part. Now, if such a person is always a pure white entity with an advanced soul dedicated to good, why was one person removed from this pursuit? I'm not sure—except that, as unusual as it sounds, this person defaulted on their promise to God. I agree that one out of thousands is an abnormality, but in all life, there are flukes that we learn from. Apparently this individual was worried about how their life was evolving, but pride and arrogance took over and they began to sink into self-deception.

If you want to become a mission-life entity, you can do so by asking God. But this means that you give your life to Him and your love affair with Him begins very intensely. If and when you do, you might find that you're called on to perform for God, but what better way to spend your life here? This doesn't mean that you have to join a convent or go sit on a rock somewhere—it just means that one way or another, you're going to do God's will. (Please note that you're either a mystical traveler or not—this is something that's imprinted on a soul and can't be requested while you're on the Earth plane.)

❧❧

In addition to mystical travelers and mission-life entities, all of the sciences are also studied and researched on the fifth level. (Although you'll find some scientists on the sixth level, most are on the fifth.) There are huge research centers in abundance on this level, wherein laboratories are making new discoveries every day.

These breakthroughs are then infused to scientists and researchers on the Earth plane to bring out to the world. The only problem is that because of the bureaucracy of the planet these "new" ideas get put on the back burner or are not funded properly. The cure for cancer, for instance, has already been discovered on the Other Side, but getting it through to the Earth plane is a long and tedious process.

There's a lot of interaction between the scientists on this level and those on other levels. Scientists in drug research consult with marine biologists and herbalists on the third level constantly, and researchers in the physical sciences will consult with mechanical engineers and gemologists. There's no jealousy, academic prejudice, or fear of a discovery being usurped, because everyone is working together for the common good.

There are also counselors on this level who work with children who are either coming Home or going out to a life on Earth, and they interact freely with those on the sixth level who deal with trauma and adult souls. I have to emphasize that those on the Other Side are the epitome of teamwork as they pull together for the common good of creation and God. It's truly a joy to work in the field of your choice without all of the human subterfuge and egos that we encounter on Earth. There's no commuter traffic, no time cards to punch, and no need to worry about promotions and salaries, since there isn't any currency here.

In other words, you can fulfill your passion for a particular field of endeavor without all the hassles and influences that a career brings on Earth. You have any materials that you need; you travel for fieldwork by thinking yourself to your destination; you have every piece of machinery that you require; and you can even make new, inventive equipment if necessary without having to worry about a budget. It's truly the ideal setting in which to devote yourself to doing what you love and taking full advantage of it.

CHAPTER 15

THE SIXTH LEVEL—
TEACHERS AND LECTURERS

The sixth level is where we find teachers, lecturers, and more counselors. And although there are researchers on every level, most of them are actually on this one. They may choose to study any subject they want in the plentiful laboratories or research centers here—many who explore topics such as history or theology, for instance, do so in the Hall of Records. Francine says that this building is so vast that you really have to know what you're looking for. Thankfully, helpers that function like librarians are available to direct you to specific areas and assist you in pulling the information you need. This incredible edifice even houses the charts of every life we've ever lived and outlines them in the greatest detail.

Teachers and lecturers also reside on every level, but again, the bulk of them are here on the sixth. They share their lessons with all to enjoy and learn from while on the Other Side, but of course this doesn't mean that these entities are advanced above any others; rather, it's just a delineation of one's chosen vocation. The inhabitants of this level have elected to aid people coming in and out of incarnations as well as those on the Other Side. And the counselors here take on the "hard cases" of both incoming and outgoing souls, helping those who are about to enter a difficult life as well as those who have just come from one.

❧❦

The sixth level is also the one in which we're taught how to be spirit guides. There's a more than 98 percent chance that we'll be (or have been) a guide, regardless of what level we're on. It's almost like a reciprocation of sorts, an example of "I'll help you and then you'll help me." Yet this isn't as easy as it sounds, as we'll spend a great deal of effort, and what we'd relate to as time, to learn the specifics of being a spirit guide to someone. As we watch over our charge, our normal activities on the Other Side are put aside somewhat until he or she comes back Home. However, it's only like a few weeks to us, and it's no great hardship (except, perhaps, in the special case of having to look after someone who has a particularly difficult life to complete).

Some guides, like Francine, have to undergo advanced training because they're "communicating guides." This means that they convey information through their charges, thanks to mediumship abilities like mine. Such guides also have to learn how to communicate verbally or audibly (in my case), learn how to telepathically channel more strongly, or discover how to occupy the body (also in my case) of the medium they're in tune with. Yet *all* guides have to get messages or warnings across. They also have to go through extensive preparations to become more "humanized"—otherwise, they couldn't really empathize with Earthly plights.

Francine has mentioned to me many times that she's heard a marvelous speech or lecture, or she took a class from Aristotle or Benjamin Franklin or some other fantastic historical figure. Now you might ask, "How can my guide be by my side always, yet still be able to go to all these lectures or classes?" Well, remember that everyone can bilocate on the Other Side. This means that our guides can be with us even as they're absorbing an event or doing something at another location.

My spirit guide, for instance, researches creation and different religions for me, which has certainly helped with the Society of Novus Spiritus. She'll consult with others who are learned in the particular field she's researching, and oftentimes she'll tell me where I can find information on my own plane to verify it or make reference to it. Even as all of this is done, she never leaves me alone—just as your spirit guide is constantly with you and devoted to you.

Francine has also told me that the instruction and lectures that go on at Home are the most inspiring and that the music is truly heavenly. She's explained that they have many festivals over there that celebrate events like our Christmas, or they might have many celebrations depending upon how many lives someone has led— or just one to commemorate them all at the same time. (These large celebrations are usually organized by sixth-level inhabitants.) An entity may also choose to observe its own special day, such as graduating back to the Other Side after death on Earth. This would be akin to our Earthly birthdays, because coming back Home is truly the day of being born back into our real life.

Spirit guides, researchers, and teachers confer with the Council frequently when they need help. For example, a spirit guide might ask for the Council's assistance when the person they're guiding gets into trouble. They don't interfere, but many times they try to telepathically help their charge with tough decisions or through grief or adversity. I guess you might say that they're the advanced therapists and problem solvers of the universe.

There are many ways to attack an obstacle, and some are better than others. When I get confused, I ask Francine to confer with the Council about my Society, study groups, or even my own life. The answers she brings me often make me say, "Why didn't I think of that before?!" When I was going through my last divorce and was in pain from so much deception, for instance, I asked for help. Almost immediately, a lightning bolt of sorts struck my mind and began to form a montage of thoughts of so many things I didn't see, such as my ex's caustic secrecy, jealousy, and need to take control . . . and once my intellect saw this, my pain diminished. Knowledge always sets us free.

So here again, I'm amazed and sometimes amused that people feel as if they're so alone when they actually have so many loved ones around them constantly who want to help. You need only ask, and a task force of assistance will be on its way!

CHAPTER 16

THE SEVENTH LEVEL— BACK TO THE GODHEAD

The seventh level can be really confusing, as it's the one where people give up their individuality and go back into the Godhead (that is, the uncreated mass of God). This is an uncommon experience, as I've only met one person in all the readings that I've done who was on this level. He was a priest, and the head of a theology department at a university, who told me that he didn't want to keep his identity; instead, he wanted to go back into God.

I'm sure that some Buddhist monks or Hindus also aspire to become part of the wonderful heart or mind of God that created them. After all, the term *nirvana* has often been used for the state of being at one with God. Certain religions believe that to attain this state means to perfect one's soul through the living of enough lives—and by becoming one with God in eternal bliss, they don't have to endure any more Earthly existences. But we can do so without losing our Divine identity . . . and most of us do just that. (Even with all of his magnificent evolvement, Jesus is still in his glorified body at Home.)

Here again, it just proves that we have free-will choice on the Other Side: We pick what level we want to be on, what we want to do, and how many (and what kind of) lives we want in order to perfect and experience for God. We may even choose to go to other planets and incarnate on them if we feel that it will advance our soul. We have many options to select from, but it's all done voluntarily, and it's all done on the Other Side.

So while the rest of us on the other levels keep our own identities and go about our business—whether it's to live lives, work, or research—those entities that elect to go to the seventh level lose their individuality and identity but aren't destroyed. There's no such thing as annihilation, as everything God has ever created can never be uncreated. It may just take a different form and become a part of what we might call the "collective consciousness."

Francine says that the collective consciousness of all those who have been reabsorbed back into the Godhead can be used as an effective tool for help. Those on the Other Side refer to it as the place of the "veil," and to go behind it means to seek aid from that consciousness. She also told me that not many entities avail themselves of this assistance . . . and after she described her one and only visit there, I can understand why.

My spirit guide said that the veil is like a shimmering barrier that's beautiful to behold. When she walked through it, she was immediately confronted with a sight that wasn't necessarily frightening but disconcerting: Millions of faces seemed to be staring at her, and all communication was done telepathically with what seemed to be tremendous resonance. It was almost as if echoes were resounding inside her mind. Although it was a unique and uplifting experience for Francine, it was also somewhat alien. I can certainly understand why she hasn't gone there again, as well as why so many choose not to go at all. With her description of so many faces there, perhaps there *is* a type of individuality kept within God's essence.

I love God with my very soul and have given my life to Him, but I don't choose to go into the seventh level. I sometimes can't wait to go Home—it's not that I don't love my life, but we *all* long for that unfulfilled place that seems to reside in our soul . . . a place where we belong, and it isn't here on Earth. I don't think we ever find total peace in this life because our subconscious remembers a place that we come from, which is so perfect and beautiful that we call it Home.

So just know that, no matter which of the seven levels you choose to reside in on the Other Side, you're going to be sublimely happy.

PART IV

A New Look at Some Old Favorites

Introduction to Part IV

This next part concerns a few topics that I've approached in other books before, but not in so much depth. These are also the three subjects that I'm asked about again and again by my fans.

— First I'm going to revisit information about the 12 levels of the soul that I've received from my spirit guide Francine, as well as from my own research spanning some 50 years. Then I've opened myself up to God's viewpoint on the subject, for I feel that if we put ourselves in His position, we can comprehend things a bit better . . . or at least we'll get another perspective.

— Next, I'm going to thoroughly explore one of the most popular subjects from my books and lectures: dark entities. I guarantee that just about everything you could ever want to know about these unfortunate creatures will be explained here, by both myself and Francine.

— Finally, I'll take some time to illustrate the difference between religion (that is, dogma) and spirituality, as I feel I'm often misunderstood when it comes to these two very different pursuits.

So get ready to go on an incredible journey of discovery and wonder—namely, to know the wherewithal of our creation and purpose . . . at least to the point that our finite minds can understand it!

CHAPTER 17

REVISITING THE
12 LEVELS OF THE SOUL

Since so much of this information on the 12 levels of the soul is covered in my book *God, Creation, and Tools for Life*, I'll only present a short synopsis of each level here (which has been adapted from that book). Then I'm going to try something a bit different: I'll relate each of these 12 levels to areas in the biblical book of Genesis . . . and then I'll come back at you from the viewpoint of God. I realize that this is a bit unorthodox, but many times the best way to see and understand information is from another point of view. Since, like you, I'm a part of God, I feel that I can use my writer's discretion in this matter—besides, wouldn't you be disappointed if I wasn't a little bit controversial?

Level 1: Thoughts in the Mind of Father God

The first level of the soul has to do with the creative impulse, which is at the root of the most ancient and authentic beliefs about where we came from. The following is the closest I could get to a quote from Genesis that relates to this first level, but it does refer to the second one as well and can be used for both. Notice that here the Creator points out the fact that there is a duality—both a Father and Mother God: **Genesis 1:26–27**—"God said, 'Let us make man in our own image, in the likeness of ourselves, and let them be masters of the fish of the sea, the birds of heaven, the cattle, all the wild animals and all the creatures that creep along the ground.' God created man in the image of himself, in the image of God he created him, male and female he created them."

God's viewpoint: "You always were there residing in Me. Being the Father, I sustain all of My creation. Because everything I have made is part of Me, and each of My creations has a part of Me within them, I love you all. Humankind, you are My children, just as the planets and stars, trees and flowers, air and water, animals and fish and birds are. You are children of a different kind . . . just as creation is so diverse, so are My children unique unto themselves. Each of you has a different part of Me inside you, which makes you a special creation, for no other has the part of Me that resides inside you.

"You were created in My image and in that of Mother God— Our love for each other is your life force, and just as Our love will always be, so *you* will always be. In the true reality, there is no time or past or future, for My existence is always in the now. When you are in the true reality of what you call the Other Side, you can see past and future events because they all converge into My now. So essentially everything in creation is happening at the same time—you can even talk to yourself or someone else in what you deem the past or future.

"For finite understanding, picture time as you perceive it to be a circle with no beginning and no end, which revolves so fast that no matter where you enter, you are in all eras, centuries, decades, years, days, hours, and minutes. Your mind only focuses and exists transiently for a moment in what you would call a particular 'time' to live a life, but that is not reality. When you get back to reality and the Other Side, your mind expands and you exist in all 'times' in My now. It then becomes, in a sense, *your* now."

Level 2: The Thoughts Made Flesh

When God began to have these creative thoughts, the second level of the soul's maturity was put into being. We've always been part of God's lineage; therefore, we have His genetics. We've always heard that we were made in the image and likeness of God, but when we say that we *are* God, everybody is shocked. Why don't we carry that notion outward—not as a belief, but as rational thought?

As Francine says, "There are so many entities that are not advanced enough to comprehend this point, so it should make you very proud that you've advanced this far. But in the beginning, everyone had more or less the same aptitudes and abilities. How they used them and how they accelerated is part of their spirituality."

Again, let's look at **Genesis 1:26–27**—"God said, 'Let us make man in our own image, in the likeness of ourselves, and let them be masters of the fish of the sea, the birds of heaven, the cattle, all the wild animals and all the creatures that creep along the ground.' God created man in the image of himself, in the image of God he created him, male and female he created them."

God's viewpoint: "When Mother God and I gave each of you a form or body, you essentially became either a male or a female. You are not both, but each resides within you, just as your Mother and I do. You are all sons and daughters of Us both. Do you not see this in the natural order of things in what you call 'nature'? There is a constant duality of male and female, just as it is with your Creators.

"You are a combination of intellect and emotion: The intellect gives you a direction, while the emotion activates you to go in that direction. The balance of both gives you spirituality, and the imbalance gives you chaos. Do you not see this in the wild in how things progress to a natural conclusion? If they are out of balance, their advancement is hindered. It is the same with you— if balanced, you flourish; if you go into imbalance, you become static and fail to move forward.

"Do you not see the vastness of space and the stars? Do you not notice the limitless power and natural laws of Our creation? While on Earth, you can only view a small part of creation even with your most powerful instruments, but then you see billions of stars and tens of thousands of galaxies that contain even more stars and planets. We created all this and more, so why would you think that your Creators do not love you? What would be the point? It is why you exist! Why would you think We are so shortsighted that We would be angry, vengeful, or hateful? Do not give to Us your undeveloped human traits that have been espoused in your various religious dogmas and holy books. It is not factual, and it is not the truth!

"Do you not realize that your ideas, thoughts, and feelings are all a part of your journey to find the truth? You are infants now, and how much does an infant know? You have a few concepts of what is true, but you wallow in so much falseness that it overrides them. You are too busy fighting and killing one another and trying to subjugate others to your perceived 'truths'—whether they are religious, political, or economical—that you have no time to realize or even comprehend what is actual.

"You humans are your own worst enemy, yet you are just babies. Your Mother and I know that you will eventually learn, even if it takes eons . . . but do not think that We do not love you despite all of your infant mistakes. Do not expect Us to interfere that much in your development, for even though Mother God will intercede from time to time, She will not interfere with the overall scope of creation. You, Our created children, must learn and evolve through creation, for We cannot do it for you—but know that We *are* always there for you . . . sustaining and nourishing."

Level 3: Developing Our Themes

Here we began to compose our charts. If we write: "I'm going to be beautiful, wonderful, and wealthy; everyone will love me; and I'm going to have everything," it wouldn't add to our perfection. Only when the metal is tempered can we form it into something, so the tougher and more daring we are, the more experience we write in. But as we spend time in the physical body, we find that life on Earth is harder than expected.

The biblical passages I found relating to this level (**Genesis 2:8–9, 2:15–17, 3:1–13,** and **3:16–19**) give the basics of the "fall of man," which is really an allegorical story to explain that humankind goes into life on Earth to learn how to progress their souls despite being surrounded by negativity. In fact, the "garden" is actually a symbol of the Other Side. (You must understand that primitive humans were illiterate, so most knowledge was passed through stories and parables in order to make them understand.)

I've always questioned the view of God according to the Old Testament: He's continually being portrayed as wrathful and vengeful and constantly at odds with humankind, either disappointed in them or punishing them. I never cease to be amazed by how some people can believe every word of the Bible, and by how it's taken literally so much of the time. The so-called good book contradicts itself so many times that it's completely illogical. You can see that contradiction in some of the passages mentioned in this chapter . . . for God is portrayed as being all perfect and knowledgeable, yet He doesn't know where Adam and Eve were in the garden? Or He didn't know that they'd eaten of the forbidden fruit—or the circumstances of their decision to eat said fruit? Come on . . . give us a break here!

You can't have God asking questions, because that signifies that He doesn't know something. An omnipotent and all-knowing God doesn't ask questions, He answers them! It just goes to show that individuals have written their own words into the Bible, especially when they gave God all of these human traits. Does that mean that the Bible doesn't contain His word and truth? Not necessarily, but do realize that people have mixed in a lot of their own beliefs and words for their own purposes of religious expediency.

The one biblical passage I'd especially like to focus on is **Genesis 3:1–13**—"Now, the snake was the most subtle of all the wild animals that Yahweh God had made. It asked the woman, 'Did God really say you were not to eat from any of the trees in the garden?' The woman answered the snake, 'We may eat the fruit of the trees in the garden. But of the fruit of the tree in the middle of the garden God said, "You must not eat it, nor touch it, under pain of death."' Then the snake said to the woman, 'No! You will not die! God knows in fact that the day you eat it your eyes will be opened and you will be like gods, knowing good from evil.'

"The woman saw that the tree was good to eat and pleasing to the eye, and that it was enticing for the wisdom that it could give. So she took some of its fruit and ate it. She also gave some to her husband who was with her, and he ate it. Then the eyes of both of them were opened and they realized that they were naked. So they sewed fig leaves together to make themselves loincloths.

"The man and his wife heard the sound of Yahweh God walking in the garden in the cool of the day, and they hid from Yahweh God among the trees of the garden. But Yahweh God called to the man. 'Where are you?' he asked. 'I heard the sound of you in the garden,' he replied. 'I was afraid because I was naked, so I hid.' 'Who told you that you were naked?' he asked. 'Have you been eating from the tree I forbade you to eat?' The man replied, 'It was the woman you put with me; she gave me some fruit from the tree, and I ate it.' Then Yahweh God said to the woman, 'Why did you do that?' The woman replied, 'The snake tempted me and I ate.'"

God's viewpoint: "In keeping with the fact that We love all of Our creations, your Mother and I have a paradise for you to reside in as the real reality of your existence—that which you call 'heaven' or 'the Other Side.' Knowing that you had to learn to progress, We also realized that part of that process would be to find out about the nature of evil and negativity. Such states do not reside in your paradise of a Home, but in another dimension known as Earth. This is only a temporary dimension that, for a moment (what you call 'years'), allows you to experience that negativity in order to progress to the level of education you desire with free-will choice. In other words, you choose what level of perfection and learning you want for yourself and your soul. This also goes along with the premise that you are all unique. Each of you will not only choose a different level of learning or perfection for yourself, but you will also choose what that lesson is to encompass and how you will attain it.

"To give an analogy for your understanding, your themes are like 'majors' and 'minors' in your college-education systems—you pick particular areas to work on for your soul's progression. Since each one has infinite possibilities for diversity, it is what you call 'impossible' to attain all knowledge. You are not Us, and We don't expect that of you . . . but realize that when all of creation is put together, your knowledge is part of Our knowledge and your experience is part of Our experience. Each of you has your place in creation, and each place is unique and important. We love and cherish you all."

Level 4: Writing Our Charts

At the fourth level, each life's details are filled in. We took a theme, and we're going to perfect it as best we can in every existence. Some themes seem tougher than others, but that isn't necessarily so—they just rub every single person differently.

Our experience is a direct feedback to God, Who, in all knowingness, can't experience except through His "ten fingers" (creations). We are those fingers that move and feel. It isn't that we don't have intelligence, but rather that we're experiencing for God because we're sparks of Him. It's such an uplifting thought to note that we'll never get lost in the milieu of things—we're never going to go somewhere that we won't be noticed. As Jesus said, "Every hair on your head is numbered." Can you tell me that parents don't know the love between their children and them in Earthly life? How do you think that compares to what's between Father and Mother God and Their offspring? It's even more magnificent because of Their magnanimousness and gigantic ability to love!

There are no real references in the Bible to life themes, other than to note the diversity of occupations.

God's viewpoint: "Everything in creation is open to seekers of knowledge. As creation is so vast, so is knowledge. You have only to ask the question and then look for the answer, which is always available to those who seek.

"There is total order in creation. That order is carried down to the smallest of details, and as such, it also applies to your life themes. It gives you specific subjects to study and learn, presenting you with a curriculum of life that you can build on to perfect for your soul. Since there are so many facets to each theme, learning is not only a joy, but it also can be endless in scope. As you discover, your soul builds in stature and knowledge and truly 'dost magnify the Lord.'"

Level 5: Beginning to Experience

The fifth level is when we begin to experience; when emotion starts to separate from pure intellect. It's where our hearts begin to hurt—this is the tough level, where we separate ourselves from the giant intellect.

When you eat of the tree of knowledge, it means that you have to go down and experience. Do you not see how rational that is? Everybody said, "Oh boy, Eve sure was nasty. Wasn't she awful?" Well, she was nothing more than the symbol of emotion, but she had to be the driving force for intellect—after all, intellect by itself can do nothing. If, for example, I conceive of this book, I still need the impetus to make it a reality. Something has to be the mover.

And that brings us to **Genesis 3:22–23**—"The Yahweh God said, 'Now that the man has become like one of us in knowing good from evil, he must not be allowed to reach out his hand and pick from the tree of life too, and eat and live for ever!' So Yahweh God expelled him from the garden of Eden, to till the soil from which he had been taken."

God's viewpoint: "Knowledge can be all things, but experience is a large part of that. You can never have total and complete cognition of something until you have felt it as well as studied it. Much of your experience will be trial and error . . . with the emphasis on *error*. This does not mean that if you err you are bad or evil or negative. When you do not learn from your errors is when you truly negate knowledge and prevent it from working for you. This sets you back many times, and you have to go over the same material again and again to finally comprehend it.

"Spirituality is nothing more than an accumulation of truthful knowledge. The key here is *truthful*. You may observe what you deem to be a 'holy man' who has what appears to be a vast knowledge of spirituality, but if that knowledge is filled with untruths, then it is like dust in the wind . . . utterly useless and sometimes harmful. Do not judge to be spiritual that which through wealth or trappings have made themselves look spiritual, or teachings that condemn others to the point of inspiring hate and evil. Do not judge hypocritical religions as spiritual, as they protect themselves at all costs.

"Know that We do not need your worship and adoration and We do not want your fear of Us. Know also that We embrace your returned love. We love all of Our creations unilaterally and unconditionally, so why would you think that We would be on one side or the other in a war? Both sides contain Our beloved creations, and We do not take sides in your petty differences. Why would you think that We do not love you all? We do not punish you—you punish yourselves . . . just as you judge yourselves. We will alter creation by reabsorbing its unneeded parts, but there is no 'day of judgment,' for We hold all of you in Our hearts."

Level 6: Incarnating into Physical Lives

It was always known that the only way we were ever going to perfect was in a negative environment, because we won't be able to do so in a happy, wonderful one.

We might wonder what we were thinking about when we chose our human bodies. We may say, "Why didn't I pick a better one than this?! Why wasn't I shorter, taller, heavier, or lighter?" That in itself is something that we must overcome in the physical world. We spend so much time worrying about our nose, our eyes, or our hair—then we get older and die, and who cares? I don't think anybody is going to remember the fact that your eyes were too close together, your nose was too big, or your breasts were too small.

Since I was a schoolteacher for so many years, I love to tell this story about a little girl who couldn't find her mother. She ran through a crowd, calling out, "You have to know what my mother looks like—she's the most beautiful woman in the village!" Everybody was frantic, thinking, Who is this woman? The child said, "I'm telling you that she is the most beautiful woman. You'll know her immediately." So everybody looked for this knockout, yet nobody could find her. Then all of a sudden, a snaggletoothed, straggly-haired, babushka-clad, and very short and round woman emerged from the crowd. The little girl looked up, and her face shone. "There she is!" she cried. "Don't you see? She is the most beautiful woman in the world." And of course she was, through the eyes of that child.

Having said that, I find it interesting that according to Genesis, humans once lived to be hundreds of years old. Then we come to this particular part in which God puts a limit on the number of years lived. **Genesis 6:1–3—**"When people began being numerous on earth, and daughters had been born to them, the sons of God, looking at the women, saw how beautiful they were and married as many of them as they chose. Yahweh said, 'My spirit cannot be indefinitely responsible for human beings, who are only flesh; let the time allowed each be a hundred and twenty years.'"

God's viewpoint: "By giving you free will, your Mother and I opened you up to the learning process. Most of you chose to acquire knowledge in many areas, and part of that process was to incarnate on the Earth plane or the negative planes of other planets. Such places are the only areas where negativity and evil reside. Since negativity is part of knowledge, it normally manifests itself in emotion. Our creations are nothing if not emotional—each of you has intellect and feeling within you, and as you are in the state of infancy in the learning process, emotion rules more than intellect on these negative planes.

"To incarnate on these negative planes is tough. You are subjected to this 'school' for only a moment in the scheme of eternity, but it does have a profound effect on your souls and your learning. Our love for you makes it a limited experience as far as your concept of 'time' is concerned, for just as you who are parents love your children and try to protect them, so do We. We know that you have to experience the unpleasant side of knowledge to learn from it, just as you have to watch your children experience pain and hurt and making mistakes. Just remember that it is all transient, and you will return to your paradise of a Home after living your life (or lives) on Earth."

Level 7: Dark Entities Manifest

Francine has told me that "the seventh level—and seven is a very powerful number—is where we began to see some entities 'slipping through the cracks.' After incarnation, some entities began to negate either their emotional or intellectual sides, feeling that they were so evolved that there was nothing beyond themselves."

I cover dark entities in detail in the next chapter, but here I will say that everybody has the option to be a dark, gray, or light entity. And **Genesis 6:5** states: "Yahweh saw that human wickedness was great on earth and that human hearts contrived nothing but wicked schemes all day long."

God's viewpoint: "There is a dark aspect that resides in creation, which your Mother and I allow to manifest and evolve. However, We did not create it—it was done by Our creations with the free will that We gave them. We have complete knowledge of evil, but that does not make *Us* evil. It is the same as when you know how to shoot a gun and that it will kill, that does not make you a murderer. Realize that evil and negativity only reside in the unreality of transitory dimensions—the *real* reality of eternal life is a paradise . . . the Other Side that We created for you.

"Evil and negativity are parts of knowledge that you must learn to perfect your own souls. You discover not only how to fight against evil, but also to survive residing in it. It gives you a different perspective of knowledge and how it can be manipulated. It is needed in your 'curriculum' of knowledge . . . almost like a mandatory subject for a major in college. When it is no longer necessary, We will reabsorb it back into Us, for it will have served its purpose."

Level 8: Becoming Aware of Our Identities

This level is about realizing our identity, that we're made up of intellect and emotion. The only true identification lies not in social behavior, but in the fact that we are a direct part of God's intellect (here experiencing through our dear Blessed Mother).

This is the identity that we must know because everything in life passes away, except for the love that we have for each other— that's the one sustaining thing that we have. Possessions become old or worn-out, so how we identify ourselves can only come from the love we have of God and each other, and from knowing why we're here. Each and every one of us is God . . . we must be. The same as our sons or daughters are products of us, we are the product of God. That's the greatest identity we can have.

There isn't really anything in Genesis that refers to becoming aware of one's self. We do have some analogies, however, that point to a renewal of purpose and being: There's God destroying all living things through the great flood, except for Noah, his family, and at least two (male and female) of each creature on Earth; Noah and God establishing a new covenant for humankind; and agreements with Abraham and others.

God's viewpoint: "It is always a pleasure for Us to see Our creations discover new things, especially to define themselves. You are essentially establishing a contract with Us to live and experience for Us in your learning process. This agreement brings you closer to Us, for although We never move away from you, some of you move away from Us.

"As your soul progresses through the accumulation of knowledge, you will learn more about your Creators and yourself. It is a joyous process that is never ending and filled with grace."

Level 9: A Fork in the Road—
Do We Keep on Incarnating?

As Francine explains, "The ninth level is very important and definitive, because at that point, after you have lived several lives (usually it's about five) you decide, right then, whether you're going to take on more or stop. Numerology has an ancient belief in the number nine, which is considered to be very high-blown, high-flown spirituality. The reason that nine is so ingrained as a highly spiritual number is because the soul actually picks to go on further for its own spirituality on the ninth phase.

"The ninth level is almost a bail-out or exit level. Do you want to go on? There is certainly no stigma to exiting. Many have said, 'That's it. I don't want anymore.' Some entities will stop on five (or even two or three) on one planet, but choose to go on and finish the rest on another. People are very territorial and usually become accustomed to a planet, bad or good, so they keep incarnating to perfect on it—they can become almost victimized in their attachment. You certainly cannot blame people for staying because it might take 120 lives on another planet to do what would take them only 3 here. So it's more common to go through a few very hard existences than to take on over a hundred benign ones."

In other words, the higher the level of pain—the higher our level of loving and experiencing—the stronger that fencepost holds. If we were to add one drop of red food coloring to a pitcher of water, that drop would turn the water a slight pink, but the more drops we added, the deeper the color would become. So each lifetime is a drop in the "water" of your existence. Now there's certainly nothing wrong with having a few lives—after all, Francine only had one existence on Earth. She told me that we can either incarnate here or work through our perfection by being a spirit guide. I imagine that, in retrospect, she would have rather lived many lives than be my guide! In fact, I once asked her if she ever wanted to be anybody's guide again, and she said no. That gives you a good indication.

Again, there's no specific passage in the Bible that correlates with deciding to live multiple lives, but consider this: After the great flood in Genesis, supposedly no one was left on Earth except for Noah, his three sons, and their families. And then, within a comparatively short period of time, there were thousands upon thousands of people inhabiting the planet again, founding large nations and scattering all over the globe. The Bible is nothing if not illogical at times, and this is a prime example—it simply doesn't make sense that so many people would inhabit so much area again in such a short period of time. Just as the sons of Adam and Eve found wives (where did they come from?) in another land, so it is with the repopulation of Earth after the great flood. We have to look at the Bible as a collection of stories that could explain to a basically uneducated populace how things progressed in creation, and the Book of Genesis aptly puts that forth.

God's viewpoint: "As creation progresses, so does learning. You started by learning your ABCs, and now you are into theoretical sciences that can boggle the mind. By giving you multiple lives to live, your Mother and I have presented you with the opportunity to learn as much as possible through experience. You can read about something in a book, but until you have actually gone through it, you have not learned everything.

"Now it is illogical to think that each of you will learn everything there is to know, but you *will* become a part of that overall knowledge. In other words, each of you will be a piece of the pie that encompasses all cognition. Some of you will be a slice that's smaller in size than others, depending upon how much you want to learn, but I cannot emphasize this strongly enough: *All of you are important and unique, and without you the pie is not complete.*

"Multiple incarnations give you the opportunity to experience different facets of the same thing. For example, take physical death, which will happen to you all. You may pass peacefully in your sleep in one life, or go violently in another. You may survive the death of an infant in one life, and the passing of a grown son or daughter in another. You will each undergo different aspects of the same type of experience . . . then, as your individual sparks come together, you will all make a huge dent in the infinite possibilities of any event.

"Do you also not realize that multiple incarnations explain the inequities in life? Do you think that We are so heartless and unfeeling that We would allow some to suffer while others do not? Through multiple incarnations, you can experience what your own free will wants by learning and helping others learn, too. Each of you has the opportunity to be rich or poor, to die early or live a long life, to be healthy or ill, and on and on it goes. It is your individual self that chooses what you want to experience—We have nothing to do with it.

"As your accumulated learning progresses your soul, you usually decide to make your experiences more difficult. Just as school has harder and harder subjects to learn as you move through your education process, so it is for your soul on Earth. We know that it is difficult, but you must realize that it is you who chooses to do this for the love of Us. In turn, We love you back a thousandfold and give you grace . . . which most of you in life do not even realize. It is only when you go Home that you reap this realization. There you will feel Our love in all its glory and know the happiness of paradise."

Level 10: Choosing How Much to Open Up to Knowledge

Now, the tenth level is very interesting, for we get to pick how much knowledge we want. I know this is true in my heart—I think I've been around long enough to see it—that some people really go at life on full tilt. Sure, you might get smashed up a little, but wouldn't you rather know that you really *lived* when you get to the end of the trail?

The other extreme would be very much like if I said, "All right. We're all going to Egypt, but we're just going to stay in our hotel rooms when we get there." I actually did take a group to Egypt, and I had people who did just that. I felt like saying, "I took you all the way across these continents, and now you're just going to stay in your room?" And that's what some individuals do in life. They come into their body, but they don't go out and experience. They say, "Oh, but I'm scared! What if I change jobs or move and it doesn't work? What if I can't make it in this marriage?" So what?! Unless you take chances, you experience nothing.

People say, "But what if I die?" Well, that's the one thing we're all going to do. We could be sitting in our house and the whole roof could cave in on us. So it would be nice to be able to lie on our deathbed and say, "I did it all! I grabbed every ring I could." Personally, that's the knowledge that I came in for—I want my soul to expand.

You know the Catholic prayer that contains the line "My soul doth magnify the Lord!"? Well, how do you think your soul gets larger? How do you think your cup runneth over? Only if you experience! And don't gripe about it—there's nothing worse than walking down the street with people who are whining, "I don't want to do this, and I don't like that." They're just a nightmare, aren't they?

Francine says, "We're seeing so many people in this world getting to a point in which they've done all the wonderful, technical, great things they were supposed to do. Whether they were lawyers, merchants, or tailors, at some point they became terribly burned out. The reason is because they were at such a high perfection level—the tenth level—that they realized they were too open and needed to close off. However, this could be averted by getting to a place of spirituality, wherever that may be for you."

I won't quote any Bible verse here, for it would take up too much room, but you might want to consider the story of Sodom and Gomorrah **(Genesis 18:16–33, 19:1–29)** as a tale that outlines the difference between evolved and unevolved souls. I also find it interesting here that Abraham negotiates with God in trying to save the two cities from being destroyed because there might be people living there, namely Lot and his family. As you probably know, they escape the cities as they're being destroyed by God, and Lot's wife looks back—even though she was told not to by God's angels—and is turned into a pillar of salt. The tragedy here is that God is again portrayed as vengeful, wrathful, and destructive. Why does humankind attribute their faults to Him? This "holy book" is filled with countless instances of this. What a shame!

God's viewpoint: "By giving you free will, Mother God and I allowed you to choose whether or not you wanted to become more evolved. We love our creations no matter what their choices, and We allow those that are unevolved and even those that have turned dark to mix with the evolved souls on Earth. This is the only plane where evil is allowed to coexist with good, and there is a reason for this. The temporary Earth plane is a school to learn about negativity, which is part of knowledge. In Our love for creation and Our children, We only allow evil and negativity for that purpose and that purpose only.

"The terms *evolved* or *unevolved* are really misnomers, since We are only talking about different levels of knowledge obtained by individual entities. Would We love a child who has a high school education any less than one who has graduated from college? You often speak in terms of attainment and place too much importance on it. You, of course, are only being human and again do not see the larger picture of things. Some of Our children were created with greater knowledge in order to give wisdom and help to others, but because We created them that way does not make them better. They had no hand in it—We did. To have order, certain things must exist to maintain it, and these created entities help do just that. Are they beloved by Us? Certainly . . . but then so are all of you."

Level 11: Going Home

This level marks the end of the cycle of human lives as we know it. We go Home . . . and isn't that a wonderful thing? Every once in a while we meet someone here on Earth and feel a connection—we know that there was a preordained reason that we were to come together for that brief moment, and we have a sense that we're home. That's what going to the Other Side feels like—pure euphoria, as if we could go forth and conquer the world. Nothing is going to be as bad as what we've already faced, and we can still love God through it all and be warriors for Him. We'll spend our time on Earth, see the sights, and then go Home.

The Old Testament (which includes Genesis) doesn't refer to heaven or the Other Side except as God's kingdom. You must realize that this portion of the Bible is basically Judaic in nature, which is why references to paradise are practically nonexistent. Such individuals were more concerned with continuing their lineage of dynasties through their descendants until the "day of judgment." However, there *are* numerous references made to heaven and paradise in the New Testament by Christ. Here's one of my favorites: **Matthew 19:13–15—** "People brought little children to him, for him to lay his hands on them and say a prayer. The disciples turned them away, but Jesus said, 'Let the little children alone, and do not stop them coming to me; for it is to such as these that the kingdom of heaven belongs.' Then he laid his hands on them and went on his way."

God's viewpoint: "To believe that your only existence is on Earth is to ignore all the truth that is there for you to see. Do you think that the little baby who dies only has a few moments of life? What would be the point in this being true? Do you think that Our energy and sustenance is so shallow?

"Your Mother and I made creation to exist, not to be destroyed or ended in the twinkling of an eye! We created a reality that is a paradise . . . and it awaits all who have not turned away. *We* never turn away, but your free will allows you to. You do not need to fear Us, for that is against what We are: pure love. You cannot fear something and love it at the same time, for fear is a negative emotion and love is a positive one.

"You who are preached at to fear Us, put earplugs in your ears! To fear Us is not the way to Us—but love is! Love each other and your Creators, and your spirituality will be manifested. To let fear or any other negative emotion in is to close the door on the truth and lessen your capability of spirituality.

"Your existence is assured, and even those who have turned away will not be destroyed but absorbed. This schematic that you are in is one in which knowledge about negativity and evil is learned, but it is not the permanent reality of the Other Side—a place that has no negativity and where evil is not permitted to exist. Did you not think that there would be a place for you to call Home? Did you think that Our love for you would not prepare a Home for you that is beautiful, peaceful, and full of joy and happiness? Know that We love you all and that there is a place for you to reside in with Our love surrounding you always."

Level 12: Resuming Life on the Other Side

Knowledge aids us along the path to enlightenment. Do you know what enlightenment meant to Siddhartha Gautama, the Buddha? Knowledge! It did not mean sitting cross-legged in a corner and chanting—it meant reading, studying, learning, thinking, and reasoning. And in **Luke 11:9,** our Lord said, "Ask and it will be given to you; seek and ye shall find; knock and it shall be opened unto you!"

Most of the world's "holy books" were written many years ago and were intended for an uneducated populace. Again, the Bible has no passages that refer to the premise of going Home, but neither does any so-called holy book. I've often wondered why religion doesn't update their teachings like science does. At one time they believed that the world was flat, but then they corrected themselves when the truth was discovered. Why doesn't religion do that? Is it tradition? Fear? Control? Yes—it's all of those and more. Their leaders are so comfortable in their niches of riches and control that they certainly don't want to rock the boat or kill the goose laying the golden egg.

We're supposed to believe that we had prophets and messengers for thousands of years, and then all of a sudden they stopped? Well, they didn't . . . and the number of freethinkers grow every day because dogma has failed to give us the answers we seek. This is why I (and so many others) write, lecture, and teach. Truth is truth, and it will get out despite all of the machinations by religions to suppress it.

As I explain in detail in Chapter 19, I think that parts of religion are wonderful and beautiful, and I ask that you use your mind and think. You don't have to buy everything that *anyone* tells you—pick and choose what you're comfortable with and discard the remainder . . . just as you should with my writings. I won't be offended, and I won't curse you or stop loving you for it. So why would God do any less?

God's viewpoint: "When you choose not to incarnate anymore, you naturally want to go back to the Home that awaits you. Each planet in the universe that is inhabited has its own Other Side, so you migrate back to that of your home planet. If you have chosen Earth as your home planet, do know that in the final schematic of creation, all of the Other Sides of all the planets will merge into one final dimension of beauty, harmony, peace, and happiness."

꿍꿍 꿍꿍

CHAPTER 18

DARK ENTITIES EXPLAINED ONCE AND FOR ALL

It is now time to discuss one of the things I'm most often asked about: the role of dark entities in creation. It's hard for our finite minds to comprehend, but let's say that in the beginning, God created some souls with more knowledge than others to aid the rest of us. This group of entities would include members of the Council, mystical travelers, and mission-life entities. The rest of us, on the other hand, were given very little knowledge so that we could evolve at our own pace. Thanks to our free will, we'd be able to attain the level of individual evolvement that we'd chosen for ourselves.

Only God truly knows how negativity and evil came into being, but I have a pretty good idea how it happened, and Francine concurs. (More of her views on the subject appear in her own words at the end of this chapter.) As was explained in the last chapter, negativity is part of total knowledge, and as such, it had to come into existence at some time or other in order for created entities to learn about it and evolve. In other words, God knew that evil would be instigated by those who had free will . . . which means us.

Whether this negativity started while we were still orbs of light or it waited until we obtained bodies doesn't really matter. The point is that, thanks to the combination of emotional makeup and free will, some entities allowed their own egos to override their intellects, causing a separation from God.

This rift caused the entities to become dark. With ego and visions of grandeur fueling them, they opted to gain power in any way they could. They wanted to rule their own destinies, thinking of themselves as good as, or even better than, their Creators. (The irony here is that we all rule our own destinies and don't have to become evil or negative to do so.) With power comes corruption and ego gratification; consequently, acts of cruelty and intimidation started taking place among those who lived on the early planets, either spurred on or actually perpetrated by these entities who decided to separate from God. It was their way of obtaining power and holding on to it.

It's interesting that the dark entities have made their own sort of reality. Just as we can create things from our thoughts on the Other Side (such as buildings or homes), dark entities have created a place of residence for their hierarchy. Normally they keep reincarnating on the planets that they use as their home base, so to speak, but they also created a place in an alternate dimension for their leaders to dwell in. They call it *Noir*, which means "dark" or "black," and it's almost their answer to God's creation of the Other Side. Noir is a singular planet that doesn't have the magnificence and beauty of the Other Side—in fact, I understand that it's very dreary. We know little about it, as naturally no one wants to go there, but I've been told that it will also be absorbed in the end schematic.

In addition, the bulk of dark entities are somewhat primitive in nature. I don't mean that they lack intelligence, but that they act on their base emotions of lust, power, corruption, cruelty, and the like in creating as much turmoil as they can. They've essentially devolved into chaotic entities that put forth negativity and evil in their actions to conquer God and His creations.

Most dark entities can be easily discerned, for they live only for themselves and their own gratification. It's all about them, and everyone else can go to hell. In some instances, however, they can be hard to recognize. They hide themselves behind a smoke screen (usually in a religious or political arena) and put themselves forth as leaders or individuals of great wisdom . . . and then they proceed to instill hate, bigotry, and prejudice in those who listen. They're hypocrites of the highest order, and their "teachings" only serve to spread their lies to the world.

Dark entities can be very cunning in that they seem to maintain a false front that can manifest in a delightful personality or even a charisma that can entice many to follow them. Think of Adolf Hitler, Jim Jones, or Osama bin Laden —individuals who were able to lure their followers into performing acts of cruelty and evil for their own ego gratification, using either a religious or political agenda for their own ends. Yet dark entities can come in all shapes, colors, and genders—they can be blatant or subtle, vicious or seemingly kind, stupid or seemingly wise, selfish or seemingly magnanimous. In other words, they can be lions in sheep's clothing, but they can't be spiritual like white entities. They also can't or won't love God, although many do put that facade forth.

The dark ones can physically hurt you when you're incarnate, such as through spousal or child abuse. For example, my own mother almost burned off my foot by running scalding-hot water over it. I can remember trying to hold myself up on one foot and screaming. I'm sure that it would have gone on except as God (or my chart) would have it, my aunt and uncle showed up. Today I look back and think of my mother without any hate, and I realize that she was just dark and sociopathic—and she just couldn't love.

However, dark entities' forte is to psychically attack you in your emotions. In fact, psychic attack is one of the main reasons for so much of the illness and depression in the world. I don't mean that the dark ones possess you or anything like that, but their energy, combined with the negativity of the Earth plane, is absolutely behind a lot of the anxiety and despair that goes on with humankind. But remember that the negative ones can't really hurt your soul, and that God loves all of his creations . . . even the dark entities.

☙ ❧

Now I'd like to revisit that phenomenon called the "devil." Also known as "Satan" or "Lucifer," the devil was constructed by humankind to keep people in line and controlled by religion. The whole concept of Lucifer probably came from the hierarchy that dark entities have. Those that rule the dark would be intelligent, very appealing outwardly, and certainly quite cunning.

It's interesting to note that in its etymology, *Lucifer* means "light" plus "to bear," which would translate as either "light bearing," "light to bear," or "light bringer." We were all created with the light of God within us, so essentially all of us are "beings of light." Of course dubbing the leader of the dark "Lucifer" is nothing if not ironic; however, negative entities have the attitude that they're better than God, so they feel that they're the true beings of enlightenment. We read about how Lucifer was an angel of light that fell and was condemned to hell by God with all his minions. Once again, this is just an analogy to explain the separation of the dark ones from God. And it's interesting that the so-called devil isn't actually a creation of God, but rather a construction of thought from humankind.

In years past, so-called bad spirits were blamed for all negative things, even illness. Demons were supposed to enter the body and cause it to fall sick, which is where the ancient belief and practice of bleeding came from . . . it was supposed to get rid of the "bad humors" causing illness. As different cultures absorbed beliefs from each other (as they were wont to do in ancient times due to being conquered by other countries or empires), such notions changed.

A demon became the evil Jinn, who turned back into a demon again, and then we finally ended up with a devil—or, as the Bible puts forth, an "adversary." Churches began to capitalize on this fear of the devil, which was really just supposed to symbolize negativity in the Bible as well as all the so-called bad luck that people experienced. But again, I must stress that, just as there is no hell (except for life on this planet), *there is no devil*. Period!

Q & A with Francine

The following are questions regarding dark entities that have been answered by Francine. (Most of this material has been adapted from my book *God, Creation, and Tools for Life*.)

Q. At creation, was everyone made a white entity?

A. In God's mind, yes. When His thoughtforms became flesh to experience for Him, each one made its decision to be dark or white at that exact moment.

I don't mean that dark entities just denied God, for we've seen atheists who are purely white entities. You might ask, "How can a white entity be atheistic?" Well, an atheist doesn't tend to go along with religious dogma, but you'll rarely find one who doesn't believe in *something*. Unfortunately, his or her "god" is often only power, money, or the self.

We do see entities turning either dark or light and never going back. Yet some couldn't decide, so we call them the "gray entities." They didn't know whether to be white or dark, so they chose neither. Being gray lets them sit on both sides of the fence . . . they get to be a little bad and a little good. You may say, "Well, we're all like that." Not really—they're more destructive. When you ask, "Well, why are they so good most of the time, but then they did this awful thing?" you're perfectly describing a gray soul.

Q. *What is the nature of gray entities?*

A. We generally lump them in with the dark ones. In fact, I think I actually like the darks better than the grays because fence-sitters worry me. At least with dark entities, you're very aware, almost from first contact, that they're evil. You don't have to make any decision about what you're going to do—you back up, your hair stands on end, and you feel totally put off and repulsed. Gray entities have a coaxing, almost seductive and maniacal way of pulling you toward them, as they're so wheedling, hypocritical, and deceptive. With the dark ones, you almost have to admire their dedication because they're totally committed to themselves. But you never know exactly where you stand with the grays because *they* don't know where they stand. So they're the most frightening. The unfortunate part about this is that far more grays turn black than white.

Q. *What is the percentage of black, gray, and white entities on Earth?*

A. About 70 percent gray and black, and 30 percent white.

Q. *Is being dark irreversible?*

A. Yes, it's a totally irrevocable decision, yet the ones you have to worry about the most are the gray entities, which can be beguiling and wily because they're indecipherable. There's no discerning exactly what decision they'll make at any given time, and you can't track them. The dark ones are easier to follow because they're left to come back into life after life.

Q. Are there dark entities on other planets?

A. Yes, but not like on Earth, since most entities decided that this planet was the best one to go to in order to perfect certain themes. In other words, if you wanted to be an actor, you'd go to the Lee Strasberg Theater Institute, while to pursue law, you'd go to an Ivy League college. You'd go to the best if you really wanted to hone yourself, and white entities bit off more than they could chew. You see, what's so awful about this planet is that the whole place has a terrible time being charted, individually and collectively. For example, let's say that you're going to the Amazon and you got some shots to protect you from various jungle viruses. Then, once you got there, you found out that those shots will do you no good because the viruses have mutated and there's no cure. That's what Earth is like.

You were told specifically when you came down here that all bets were off, since any planet with so many dark entities can't be charted. We on the Other Side knew that we could help you somewhat—we could try to "push your canoe" a little—but this is such a negative planet, and those dark souls play by their own rules.

Q. Do dark entities have their own Other Side?

A. No. As Sylvia previously mentioned, they have a place of residence for their hierarchy, but most dark entities reincarnate immediately upon death. It's strange, though, because their residence seems to have been created after everything else was. Now some theologians on the Other Side have said that it was always there but it just wasn't inhabited. But I feel that if it *was* always there, then they must have known that somebody was going to end up there.

Q. Are dark entities a slip in God's thinking?

A. In all thought processes, there's always that possibility, and I'm certainly not questioning God because I have such a devotion to both our Mother and Father—but God's thought process encompasses everything that humankind could ever or will ever think, and so much more. So if that's true, then there had to be dark thoughts. Just as in your own subconscious, a darkness lies within God that isn't created by Him. You should never worry about that . . . but there *is* an antithesis to Him that the dark entities represent, very much like a cancer cell.

I don't ever want to make you think that our Maker has ever done anything accidentally . . . so I know for a fact, definitively, that God allowed or put in motion the dark ones to be an antithesis for us.

Q. What is the purpose of dark entities?

A. For everyone to gain experience. Without the dark or gray souls on this planet, you'd never have anything to bounce off of.

Now why would someone like Ted Bundy, who looked all right, become a serial killer? You could have sat in a class with him, and he would have seemed like a nice, polite man. Well, the soul chooses from the very beginning, and every wrong or evil stems from greed, jealousy, or avarice. Dark entities can't wait to come into life because they get wealth, beauty, glamour, and everything else their out-of-control egos want. Of course that doesn't mean that everyone who attains wealth, beauty, or glamour are dark entities—some just felt that they'd rather be "top dog" on the wrong side than just a small light on the right one. Yet they didn't realize that, in the big picture, their little light actually would have been brighter and more powerful in the long run.

Q. Do dark entities fear losing their identity?

A. No, neither grays nor darks give it any thought. White entities always feel that way because they've fought legions of the dark ones to become their own individual parts of God. That in itself is a glorious thing. But the darks are dank and shuffle around, all looking alike . . . and they don't care.

Q. Are there also "dark angels"?

A. No, these don't exist. However, the dark residence is in a separate dimension and entirely on a lower, much more sluggish vibrational level. We spirit guides see *you* very well, but we can barely make them out. That's why it's sometimes so hard for us to protect you from them—their vibration is so slow that we can't even see them. We begin to watch you very carefully and note if you're reacting in a way in which you might be attacked, and then we start up our protection. That's why you sometimes get so mad at us and say, "Why didn't you get here sooner? Why did I have to go through this depression, this trial, this anxiety?" It's because we can hardly see them!

Q. Do dark entities have spirit guides?

A. No, they're just a conglomerate group. Whereas you have an individual guide with a name, a purpose, and a status, they don't. Dark entities do get reciprocation from their hierarchy, but they don't have a specially assigned soul that wants to protect them like you do. They're just an all-blended group that stands around as observant sentinel figures, and "psychic thugs" is the best phrase to describe them. After all, they're just down here for destructive purposes, and that's all.

Q. How about gray entities—do they have spirit guides?

A. Yes . . . but if the entity turns black, the guide immediately recedes. A spirit guide can try to take a gray and turn it white, but the minute it turns dark, the guide leaves. A gray is also allowed to select its guide. I've never been a guide for a gray entity, but I do know some guides who are, and they talk extensively with me about it. I've even merged with them to get their feelings on this, and it's so desperate.

Gray entities also do not stay on the Other Side. They go to what's called a "holding place" and get some interaction with the Other Side, but they're not allowed to reside there. They stay in the holding place because they haven't made a commitment to become white entities; therefore, they're not allowed to live at our Home.

Q. Do gray entities still get guidance from the Other Side?

A. Yes. There's counseling and, as I related earlier, they can choose a spirit guide for themselves. Special advisers from the Other Side visit them in their holding place, for a gray entity *can* turn white (although the greatest percentage of them don't).

Q. Will there always be dark entities?

A. Always, for as long as anyone incarnates. However, when that schematic has ended, centuries and centuries from the present time, there will be no use for the dark ones. I'm sure that such knowledge is only within the mind of God, relating to how much He wants to perfect His entities. Every time we guides ask, we're told that there are eons of time left, and so many entities are left to evolve.

Q. Francine, how can we cope in these chaotic times?

A. Make sure that you keep in touch with your own spirituality by being a part of some group. Without some inner golden thread, you can never feel totally comfortable. That's why everyone will eventually get into community living—it must be that way.

To strengthen your spirituality on your own, you can certainly meditate, use visualization, and envision the light of the Holy Spirit around you. Finally, set aside time to pray for, give to, and love each other, and you'll be just fine.

CHAPTER 19

DOGMA AND RELIGION

VS.

SPIRITUALITY

Whether it's the levels on the Other Side, the underworld, life on Earth, or the soul, it all points to God's magnificent order in our universe. Humankind has probed and prodded theology for thousands of years, yet most of the logic was right in front of us—usually masked by dogma and not rationale.

We on the Earth plane have unfortunately been taught that God and even Jesus, Buddha, or Mohammed are inaccessible to us . . . and I feel that this has been a huge act of cruelty to humankind. This supposed unavailability has made our Creator take on the brunt of all the sadness in our lives, or make it seem that He is absent and doesn't care. This has resulted in everyone feeling abandoned, and at one point, some even felt that "God was dead." Nothing could be further from the truth.

Even if you don't accept some (or any) of what I've related in this book, that's your own God-given right. However, I'm very sure that the more spiritual you aspire to be and the more you research, you'll come upon many of these truths, as I have. Trust me, if we study and understand more about our loving Mother and Father, it makes our life so much easier. Then we're able to realize that even with all the heartaches and suffering in our lives, our beneficent Parents are always in attendance, never wavering and always in a state of constancy, love, and protection.

It makes our lives down here in this hell so much lighter and easier to bear when we know that there's a light at the end of the tunnel—the trip back Home. Hopefully if we've learned our lessons properly, we'll never have to come back to Earth and repeat this. Some may desire to do so, but in the last 20 years I've seen more people on their last lives than I have in all of my prior 30 years of readings.

You know, when I first began to question and research, I was at times blown away . . . not just by the information I found, but how logical it was. You must realize that most of my ministers and many of my fellow Gnostic believers have been privy to this knowledge for many years, but only when the time was right did we release it. Not to take away from books like *Holy Blood, Holy Grail* or even the fictional *The Da Vinci Code* (both of which came up with some truths that had been long hidden away and suppressed from the general public), but we've had this knowledge for a considerable period of time. Not only was it handed down by channeling, but as the years went by we began to see that others had discovered Mother God, Mary Magdalene, the Dead Sea Scrolls, the Nag Hammadi writings, and numerous Sanskrit texts. In God's time, all things will come to the surface.

In this chapter I'd like to take a rational look at our world and uncover what spirituality can add to it, as well as discuss the damage dogmatic and political philosophies have done to it.

Searching for Answers . . .

Those of us who are searching for spirituality do so because organized religion has failed to give us the answers we seek. We look at this world—with its diversity of races, cultures, beliefs, and political systems—and think, *What a mess!* Now I've been lucky enough to do extensive traveling throughout many countries and to meet people in almost every culture and of every race. Do you know what I've found? In almost every instance, I've encountered beautiful and wonderful folks who were friendly, cooperative, loving, and willing to please me (a visitor) in whatever way possible. So what the hell is going on?

I have a feeling that most of the human race feels lost in many ways, so because of that, they're susceptible to influences that seem to have more knowledge and power than they do. To that end, countries' political agendas have taken precedence over the best interests of their citizens, and practiced religion hasn't budged from its dogmatic stance for centuries. No wonder people feel lost—they're not getting answers to the myriad questions that continually surface all around them, so they spiral down into a hopeless mind-set of apathy.

Most individuals can relate to the concerns of their friends and family members, but they have absolutely no idea what to do about problems on a larger scale. So they put their trust in the "powers-that-be," who just love this—because they're well aware that the majority will go along with anything they're told. We might see the occasional revolution or rare rising up of a group with a certain cause that can change a government's attitude (such as when individuals protested for civil rights or against the Vietnam war in the 1960s), but by and large, change comes hard. And when it does come, more often than not the result is a changing of one set of powers-that-be for another . . . who immediately begin dictating what *their* agenda is.

You might think that people would turn to their faith to give them solace in trying times, but that becomes a dead end as well. You see, religion does what's best for it by cooperating with governments, so it's certainly not going to jeopardize its footholds of power and stature by rocking the boat and changing the dogmatic structures that have served its ends for centuries. A primary example of this is the cooperation of churches with the Nazi regime, and certain faiths not raising an outcry against the radical factions who support terrorism and violence.

Religion in general has gotten more political in recent years, becoming more involved in the concerns of nations than ever before. Yet it's also internally polarized, to the point of being ineffective at adapting as the needs of its followers change. At this point in time, maintaining dogma is more important to religious faiths than purging what's become outdated and harmful to others. It seems that maintaining a religion and trying to make it grow is more important than the faith itself. Well, this is like spitting in the face of God and saying, "I need more followers to give me more money so that I can keep my church supported and growing. Teaching about You and helping others needs to go on the back burner."

I guess a bit of my righteous anger is coming out here because I genuinely feel that religion has failed in helping to lead people out of darkness . . . in some instances, it's actually made things darker. I'm continually confronted by people who say things such as, "Sylvia, for years I've looked to my religion for peace and solace, but it doesn't seem to care anymore," "Sylvia, my faith says to love others, but then it supports terrorism and the hurting of others," "Sylvia, my religion preaches that we should confess our sins to atone for them, yet its leaders hide their own sins and don't bring them forward," "Sylvia, my church follows Christ, who taught us to love one another and be kind to all, and then it preaches that we should condemn certain people and hate them," and "Sylvia, I love God and believe that He loves me, but my religion says that we should fear Him or He'll punish us and condemn us to hell."

I could go on and on, but I think you get the idea. People are disillusioned with their religions, and they just don't understand how their faith can say one thing and then turn around and do just the opposite.

If you look at the history of certain faiths, you'll find that they've been very inconsistent in their actions. Millions have been killed in the name of God—and it's apparent that many more will be—as the murderers are supposedly doing God's work! How hypocritical can you be? Take a stand for God, oh ye religions of humankind . . . be brave and fight against evil and negativity instead of embracing them to your bosom by perpetuating them with bigotry, hate, scandals, murder, and mayhem. You're condoning the chaos in this world by not speaking out against it.

We who are spiritual are running from you all, for you give us no solace and continue the very evil and negativity that you say you fight against! Stop the killing . . . stop covering up your internal scandals, and change your internal structure if necessary to do so . . . stop the violation of human rights . . . stop preaching bigotry and hatred . . . stop preaching to fear God and instead instruct to love Him . . . stop using your money to build ornate and overdone cathedrals, churches, mosques, temples, and the like and use the money saved for helping the poor and needy . . . stop getting into the political arenas to push your special interests forward . . . stop preaching that anyone goes to hell . . . stop being hypocrites!

Realize your failings and then correct them, be more magnanimous and tolerant toward other faiths, and take the blindfolds off to see your internal corruption and then do something about it—even to the point of abolishing traditions that sustain this corruption. Be what you're supposed to be: a voice for God to help the multitudes that need you. Know that all the negativity that survives thanks to your inaction and indifference is doing nothing but hurting those you've sworn to help.

Now, for those individuals who are working hard to effect change for the better in their religion, blessed are you in the eyes and heart of God. For all those in service to God in their particular faith, from the lowest of the low to the highest of the high, who are doing good for those they come in contact with, blessed are you in His eyes and heart. In fact, blessed are *all* who do their work for God with a pure heart and soul, only wanting to help those in need. And never think that God doesn't know what you do—be resolute and continue to serve, for change can be a long time coming, but in the end your works will always be remembered by God.

Religion in itself is not evil, but as it stands now, humankind has manipulated it to the point that many times it isn't even a faith anymore. I don't always mean to bash religion—after all, I formed a church myself—but I'd even criticize Novus Spiritus if it ever went astray. I truly believe that most beliefs mean to do good, but they get caught up in their own fear of going against what's been established before.

A religion is truly foolish if it thinks that it can get away with teaching the dogma that was originally put in place for the uneducated masses. The more informed people become, the more they will question such dogma (which tends to be contradictory to itself), and the more they'll want logical and plausible answers to their questions. Education brings with it the ability to think for oneself; consequently, questions that get answered by "matters of faith" when they have logical responses are going to bring dissatisfaction to the inquirer. Unlike the unenlightened peasant of the past, the learned person of today is searching for plausible answers and will not accept untruths.

Oh, we're always going to have what I call "herds of sheep"—those who, even if they have an education, seem to discard it when it comes to dogma. You know the type: the businessperson who attends a church that preaches "hellfire and brimstone" or the like, and doesn't even think about questioning the fact that there's a complete contradiction in having a vengeful and wrathful God in conjunction with a loving One. They can use their education in business to be very successful, but when it comes to religion, they become sheep. I've met people who are very well educated and seemingly rational and intelligent in everyday life, yet they become utterly terrified when you start talking to them about their faith.

It just goes to show you that intelligence can go out the back door when it comes to religion. Of course this is a very personal subject, so emotions can override basic intelligence in some people. When a preacher starts whipping his parishioners into a frenzy about the "wrath of God," it can be difficult to resist the infectious zealotry that goes out to the crowd and instills them with fervor.

Churches have never stopped to explain that this world of antimatter (as you know, the real reality is on the Other Side) is a place of learning for ourselves and God. Yes, we must remember that the belief systems of religion in ancient times were very primitive and basically taught by word of mouth because so few knew how to read or write—but did they forget how to *think?* Even the most ignorant peasant could observe that life contains suffering and death and start wondering why.

A Brief Look at the World's Major Religions

It's interesting to note here that all of the major religions of humankind have started from the writings of either Hinduism or Judaism. Buddhism originated from ancient Hinduism, while Judaism, Christianity, and the Islamic faith have their beginnings in the old Hebrew writings. Christianity still adheres to many Hebrew texts in espousing the Old Testament of the Bible, and it was formed from the teachings of a Jew (Jesus Christ) that were put out as a new religion by his followers and disciples. The Islamic faith follows the story of Abraham and believes him to be the father of their faith and people—they consider Jesus to be a great teacher, with the Prophet Mohammed being the last and final messenger from Allah who gave them the Qur'an (Koran).

Because of these acknowledgments, the Islamic faith believes that Allah is the same God Whom Judaism and Christianity worship (which, of course, is true).

So why is there so much dissension among these three—is it because they're rivals and interpret God differently? Surprisingly, all three religions give God human characteristics such as anger or wrath, love, jealousy, and the like; and they each recognize His power and all-knowingness. Islam places the most emphasis on God in that it acknowledges Him in all ways; Judaism does the same, but followers are also waiting for a messiah or redeemer to save them; and Christianity places most of its emphasis on Christ and the Holy Trinity (Father, Son, and Holy Spirit). All three of these religions have so much in common that their dissension clearly comes from the fact that they're rivals for followers—so they're not about to dole out much tolerance for other faiths.

The other factors that "the big three" have in common are the ancient traditions and beliefs that are ensconced in their different faiths—which inhibit their flexibility. As science has discovered, what was true ages ago is not necessarily so today; however, religion has yet to acknowledge that, so it's trapped itself into beliefs that were better suited for another time. It may have been necessary at one point to put forth a God with negative human emotions such as anger to instill fear in followers who were basically uneducated and would have reacted to these emotions. But portraying God in an untruthful and false way as a punisher Who gets angry with us may have been one of the greatest "sins" that religion has committed. Yet perhaps an even greater sin is the fact that over the centuries, religions haven't modified that depiction of God, and they've even encouraged it. It's literally "bearing false witness" . . . only it isn't to another human being, but to our Creator.

As much as I may disagree with some facets of the major religions, I also agree with many of them. Also, you can't place blame on, or be prejudicial to, any of them because it's what they believe—so if they're content with it, let it be. If we aren't tolerant, then we become no better than every other dogma that thinks it has all the right answers, and we tend to lose our spiritual belief in freedom of religion. All faiths ebb and flow and have success and failures, but God loves us all. We also have the human factor to deal with, which tends to believe that if something was in an ancient writing, then it must be true.

So again, to reiterate, no matter what your belief is, at least be lenient and positive. I say that if it's not occult, hidden, or controlling, and you're happy with it, then for God's sake—literally—stay where you are, but never be afraid to question. I came from a family that had a mixture of the Judaic and Christian religions all living in one family, and I tried even then to instill the love of God in everyone.

Some feel more comfortable fearing our Creator (which I don't agree with), but we still have to let it be. Just employ your reason and research, and you just may find that a gentler God is more plausible. Then perhaps atrocities won't be done in the name of Him—after all, since He loves us all, there could never be such a thing as a holy war.

Prophecy

Prophecy has been around as long as humankind has been in existence. It's found in the Bible, the Koran, the Talmud, and the Bhagavad Gita, as well as other writings by St. Augustine, St. Thomas Aquinas, Nostradamus, and countless others. Whether it was practiced by throwing bones, "reading" the entrails of a slaughtered pig or goat (which they still do in African cultures), or studying the stars, prophecy has been around for centuries. Asian people, for instance, have referred to the I Ching and used astrology for thousands of years to predict the future—but they've also used such pursuits to relay to others what God expected of them, to keep them from harm, or to remind them of their destinies. Even today, many Chinese won't budge into making major life decisions until they've consulted an astrologer.

Given all that, I can't believe that prophecy just up and stopped 2,000 years ago. That's like saying that we suddenly became too lowly to know, feel, or commiserate with our Mother and Father, which just isn't true. Think of life as an unpleasant camping trip, during which you contact your parents for solace because you're homesick. They console you, perhaps saying something like, "Just bear with it, honey. You're learning to be strong and independent, and you're even finding out things about yourself and what you can accomplish that you never would have had the chance to before. Besides, before you know it, you'll be home safe and proud of yourself that you got through it." And if you keep a journal yourself—that is, be quiet and ask questions—before you know it, infused, true knowledge will come through, inspired by God.

Only when someone sets himself up *as* God (like the late David Koresh or other false prophets who still abound today) do you need to be watchful and careful. Everyone is fallible except God, but your rationale will help you feel whether the words spoken or related by another are true or not. When people say that they're speaking for God, really listen to what they say—use your brain to decipher whether they're actually conveying His messages or are trying to control others with their rules and overblown egos.

False prophets exhibit obvious signs: Their way is the only way; only they know the answers; they preach fear or bigotry; they ask for your money constantly; they try to control you; they don't like answering questions, or if they do respond to your queries, it's with vague and mysterious replies that you can't understand; or they say that you must live the way they say to.

True prophets, on the other hand, are magnanimous; they care for people and their problems; are open and honest in their approach to everything; encourage learning and the study for knowledge; answer all questions in an understandable and logical manner; are loving and caring; don't force you into conversion or their belief systems; only accept voluntary contributions—and just from those who can afford it; put forth a philosophy of only an all-loving God; promote religious tolerance; fight against bigotry and hate in any form; and, most of all, are happy to help you find your own truth and way, even if it isn't theirs. I could list other traits, but you get the idea.

"Earth School"

I've always believed that this temporal plane of existence that we call Earth is a school for the soul to learn about negativity and evil and to fight against it. Religion has to find its own way, just as we individuals do. It's the experiencing of negativity that toughens the soul, and this is the only place where we'll find it. Even in Genesis, God tells Adam and Eve that they can't really taste knowledge (the symbolic apple) until they come down to Earth and work and bear children.

Our loving Father God would say: "Humankind has always tried to make My love so complicated. It is constant and never changing, even if you don't believe I am here for you. Sometimes you feel that I do not hear you or answer your prayers. I hear every word you utter and every thought you think, but like a loving parent, I cannot interfere with the lessons you have chosen for your perfection."

Know that this journey we're all on isn't about converting others—it's about revolutionizing *ourselves* from within. Now you may not agree with what I've put forth in this chapter (or in this entire book, for that matter), but when it comes to my philosophy and teachings, I've always said: "Take with you what you want and leave the rest behind." And that's what you should do with *anything*, including religion.

Afterword

As I wrote these words to you, I was in Hawaii. I was taking a little break to look out the window at the dawn, and I thought about how it gets light there so early in June. The magnitude of Francine and all the angels that I felt around me was overwhelming (as it is many times when I'm alone and contemplating), and I was also talking to my beloved father. Just then a beautiful butterfly landed on my arm. I said, "Thanks, Daddy" because I knew it was from him—he wanted to give me a little lift from the Other Side.

If you simply pay attention, you'll get signs from celestial beings. Any entity on any level of creation can visit you . . . all you have to do is ask. All your loved ones can come and give you signs, whether it's coins, birds, electrical activity, or the like. Your spirit guide can also communicate with you if you really listen, and you can ask for angels to visit and protect you. Your guide is the one that usually arranges these visits of loved ones and angels by communicating your request to them and can even bring in your totem (an animal that protects you) to protect you. Spirit guides and angels are your true companions along your journey.

You may be noticing (as many people I meet have) that time has seemingly started to speed up. It's not just if you're elderly; it happens at an earlier age now. Even my grandchildren remark about how fast summer or Christmas comes—yet when I was young, it seemed that summer vacation never came and Christmas took forever. This shows that time is hurrying up for everyone, almost as if it's condensing in this last schematic. That's why it's so important to cherish every moment with your loved ones. As my grandmother used to say, "Dirt will wait, but your children growing up so quickly won't." She didn't mean that we should live in filth, but sometimes we get too obsessive about the small stuff; and the real interactions of love, family, and friendships go by the wayside . . . never to come again. When you look at it like that, a dish in the sink can stay there.

I want to leave you with the final thought that no matter how bad life may seem at times, it's still wonderful. Regardless of what has happened to me, I've always had a really good time. (Grandma Ada used to say, "Sylvia, if ignorance is bliss, you'd be a whole blister.") Tomorrow is always a better day, and that's what has saved me. Now that doesn't mean that I haven't had pain, but I *did* see better days. I've always said to myself, "This, too, shall pass." Toothaches, childbirth, divorces, problems with the IRS—it all passes!

We can each be tubes of knowledge and healing if we just let our egos be put to the side and surrender our will to God. No one should want to be so egocentric that they want to lord themselves over others; rather, they should want to empower other people to find their own God-center. Regardless of what path we take, there are universal truths that guide us all: to do good, avoid negativity, and love God. *This is for all humankind.* "Love your neighbor as yourself" or "Do unto others as you would have them do unto you" fits into this, but I also like what Jesus said we should de when we come across negative people: "Shake the dust off your feet and walk away" and "Don't cast your pearls before swine." In other words, ingratitude, avarice, and abusive power abound in this world, but we don't have to be victimized by it.

So go forward and be a witness to your knowledge of a loving God, and I promise that the depression and despondency of this planet will begin to diminish. And don't worry if you're not always appreciated here or get the kudos you feel you deserve—God knows, and that's all that really matters.

Like Cyrano de Bergerac, all you should care about is going to God with your white plume intact (Cyrano wore a hat with a white feather). This symbolizes that you never cashed in your principles . . . and if you did or have failed (as we all do), shake yourself off, rinse your plume, and go forward. Don't get stuck in the "I could have done" or "I should have done," for that's a dead-end street. Remember that God not only knows that you're human and allows for that, but He also knows your heart and when you're trying.

Think of yourself as a spiritual warrior who can take the arrows of negativity—and even if you *are* battle worn, you'll finally reach that higher level of the soul. You'll also know how to get Home and, in the process, understand creation better than ever before.

God love you. I do . . .

Sylvia

About the Author

Sylvia Browne is the #1 *New York Times* best-selling author and world-famous psychic medium who appears regularly on *The Montel Williams Show* and *Larry King Live,* as well as making countless other media and public appearances. With her down-to-earth personality and great sense of humor, Sylvia thrills audiences on her lecture tours and has still had time to write numerous immensely popular books. Sylvia has a master's degree in English literature and plans to write as long as she can hold a pen.

She is the president of the Sylvia Browne Corporation; and is the founder of her church, the Society of Novus Spiritus, located in Campbell, California. Please contact Sylvia at: **www.sylvia.org,** or call **(408) 379-7070** for further information about her work.

NOTES

NOTES

NOTES

NOTES

NOTES

NOTES

Hay House Titles of Related Interest

THE AMAZING POWER OF DELIBERATE INTENT:
Living the <u>Art of Allowing</u>, by Esther and Jerry Hicks
(The Teachings of Abraham)

ANGELS 101: *An Introduction to Connecting, Working, and Healing with the Angels,* by Doreen Virtue, Ph.D.

ANIMALS AND THE AFTERLIFE: *True Stories of Our Best Friends' Journey Beyond Death,* by Kim Sheridan

ASK YOUR GUIDES: *Connecting to Your Divine Support System,* by Sonia Choquette

THE FOUR INSIGHTS: *Wisdom, Power, and Grace of the Earthkeepers,* by Alberto Villoldo, Ph.D.

MY PSYCHIC JOURNEY, by Chris Dufresne (Sylvia's son)

REMEMBERING THE FUTURE: *The Path to Recovering Intuition,* by Colette Baron-Reid

WHAT HAPPENS WHEN WE DIE: *A Groundbreaking Study into the Nature of Life and Death,* by Sam Parnia, M.D.

YOUR IMMORTAL REALITY: *How to Break the Cycle of Birth and Death,* by Gary R. Renard

All of the above are available at your local bookstore,
or may be ordered by contacting Hay House (see next page).

❦